MIST on
the RIVER

ALSO BY MICHAEL CHECCHIO

Sundown Legends
A Clean, Well-Lighted Stream

MIST on
the RIVER

An Angler's Quest for Steelhead

MICHAEL CHECCHIO

THOMAS DUNNE BOOKS · ST. MARTIN'S PRESS · NEW YORK

www.stmartins.com

A chapter in this book previously appeared, in somewhat different form, in the magazine *Fish & Fly*. Also, some material on salmon first appeared in *In-Fisherman*, and some material on the mythology of Bigfoot first appeared in *Gray's Sporting Journal*.

Book design by Michelle McMillian

Title page and chapter illustration by Russ Lamb

ISBN 0-312-27866-7

First Edition: October 2001

10   9   8   7   6   5   4   3   2   1

CONTENTS

MIST on
the RIVER

PROLOGUE

All across the Northern Hemisphere, salmon were late making their appointed rounds. The summer steelhead in Oregon's North Umpqua River had been delayed returning to the famous Camp Water. The steelhead hadn't shown up in any appreciable numbers even by mid-August, when the run should have been at its height. That same summer, as a killer drought and heat wave gripped the eastern Maritime Provinces of Canada, Atlantic salmon seemed to be missing in action. Halfway around the world, runs of king salmon in Alaska were behind schedule, too, as were Atlantic salmon runs in the rivers of Russia's Kola Peninsula.

That summer, Tom Pero, the publisher of a magazine called *Wild Steelhead & Salmon*, visited the famous Restigouche River that forms a border between New Brunswick and the Gaspé Peninsula of Quebec, and he wasn't able to catch a single salmon during his weeklong stay at a renowned fishing camp. Two months later, in September, Tom made his first trip to the unspoiled wilds of the Kamchatka Peninsula in the eastern wilderness of Russia to fish one of the last great runs of wild steelhead remaining on earth. Tom didn't catch a single steelhead during his week's stay on Kamchatka. In fact, he made his departure from the fishing camp on the very day the steelhead finally made their appearance.

There was nothing drastically wrong with the runs of salmon and steelhead that year. The fish hadn't swum off the face of the earth. No environmental disaster had struck the hemisphere. The fish were merely late showing up in their natal rivers. That's how it can be in sportfishing. Salmon and steelhead, attuned to subtle as well as cyclical changes affecting the planet, can't keep time according to the schedules of human beings.

"People say the steelhead are late this year," said Collin Schadrech, dipping his oars gently into the water, steadying the drift of our boat. We were gliding along on the Bulkley River in British Columbia, looking for steelhead, peering into the mirror reflection created by the timber on the banks, alert for the movements of steelhead. But what we saw mostly was the last of the spawned-out pink salmon. It was the afternoon of September 21, just a few days before the autumnal equinox.

"The steelhead aren't late," said Collin. "We're early."

Collin Schadrech operates Farwest Steelhead Lodge in Telkwa, British Columbia, on the banks of the Bulkley River, and he has been fishing and guiding steelhead anglers on his home water for the past twenty-seven years. Schadrech said the fish simply felt something in the natural cycle of season and weather that triggered their movement into the rivers this year a few weeks behind the calendar dates kept by fly fishermen.

Collin said it wasn't just the steelhead—the run of pink salmon had been delayed on the Bulkley, too. He said he noticed that the eagles began nesting later than usual and the bears weren't seen wandering down on the riverbanks at their accustomed time. Eagles feed their young on the flesh of pink salmon. Bears, whose olfactory senses are thousands of times keener than a human's, can pick up the whiff of a rotting salmon carcass miles away.

The summer had been one of the wettest in living memory in northern British Columbia. It had rained almost every day throughout the summer. And there had been a very late spring and a very heavy snowpack on the mountains. Collin told me that the Bulkley was still running a little higher than it normally would be at this time in mid-September. The Pacific Northwest was coming off a La Niña year. The cold wet currents associated with La Niña had followed a year of warm-water El Niño turbulence in the Pacific. Whatever was going on with the planet, the fish and the other animals sensed it. It was as if they were predicting long-range weather forecasts. The animals seemed to have an extension of their senses that allowed them to instinctively know things humans could only guess at. If we humans ever had that ability, we lost it long ago.

"Just look at how beautiful the water is," said Collin. "Some days you come down here and it's green. Another day, and it's like today. And the next day it's golden."

The view from the driftboat was indeed wonderful. The Bulkley was a blue-tinted snowmelt river, very clean and bright. What I look for first in a river is aesthetic beauty. Alders grew thickly along the banks, the aspens burned in patches of a scintillant September gold, and a dense forest of evergreens rose up to drink the moist Pacific Northwest air.

This was my first trip to British Columbia. I was finding it everything it was cracked up to be. For years, I had been reading about the B.C. steelhead fishing in magazines. I had gazed longingly at photographs of river bends framed by tall evergreen and mountains crowned by blue glacial ice. And I tried to imagine the freshness of those Northern scenes, the gravel bars smelling of campfire smoke and spruce after a hard rain. Searun fish were born and nourished in those Canadian waters, and they had a mystique and a beauty as spectacular as their surroundings. "Metabolism of stars, melt of snows, was shivering to its ecstasy in the steelhead," wrote the great British poet Ted Hughes.

A steelhead is a special kind of rainbow trout that migrates to the ocean when very small, and when it comes back, anywhere from one to three or four years later, it has attained the size of a salmon. Only recently have fish biologists begun to consider the steelhead as more salmon than trout, at least from the standpoint of taxonomy, and they have so classified steelhead as a subspecies of Pacific salmon. But when a steelhead comes back from the sea and enters a freshwater river to spawn, it shows its true colors, so to speak, and its oceanic silver sheen changes slowly back to its original olive-and-rainbow coloration.

And here I was, sitting in a driftboat, gliding down the Bulkley River in British Columbia, pondering the ways of steelhead, eagles, and bears.

The Bulkley was my kind of river. I like lots of mountains with my fishing, and the Bulkley had them all around, rising in one of nature's great spectacles. I prefer a big river that gives me lots of room for a backcast. Most of all, I like a river where the steelhead are all born in the gravel of the river. There were no steelhead hatcheries in this part of British Columbia. Even better, there were no dams. I like a river where a strong conservation ethic is practiced, and the Bulkley steelhead were managed strictly for catch-and-release fishing. Ranches and a few small towns appeared along the banks, but the river to my eyes still looked wild and untamed. Not exactly virgin wilderness, but the next best thing.

I could see pink salmon in the river. It wasn't a "pink year" in northern British Columbia. And yet I saw many pink salmon washed up on the riverbanks. Those salmon I spotted swimming feebly in the river were spotted all over with black patches and white fungus. The males had developed prominent humpbacks, a malformation that gave rise to their other popular name, humpies. The dying salmon had just laid their eggs in the river gravel, locking in rounds of identity, linking the generations. The nutrients they brought up from the Pacific Ocean would fertilize and power the ecosystem.

"Look over there," Collin said. A shadow passed under our driftboat. I saw a rose color within a living translucency. A very large steelhead slid under us. Collin mumbled a few words about its length and girth in inches and only afterwards did I realize he was describing a steelhead of perhaps eighteen or twenty pounds.

The steelhead were just now beginning to show up in the Bulkley behind the run of pinks. These steelhead were the reason I was here. The Bulkley River is considered by many flyfishermen to be ground zero for steelhead fishing in British

Columbia. It is world-famous, and particularly noted as the river to fish if you want to catch steelhead on dry flies.

The Bulkley is the largest tributary of a great river system known as the Skeena. The Skeena is perhaps the last grand artery for wild steelhead left in North America. Fully half of the Skeena fish pass into the Bulkley. The average size of a Bulkley steelhead is ten pounds. Each season, fly-fishermen land steelhead up to twenty pounds; a lucky few take fish over twenty-five pounds. There are even larger steelhead in nearby rivers, such as the Babine and the Kispiox. But the Bulkley steelhead are more plentiful and much more inclined to rise to dry flies; which is the apex of steelhead fly-fishing as far as I'm concerned.

Most of my steelhead fishing is done back home in northern California, so naturally I have come to think of steelhead as a notoriously difficult fish to catch. But nothing could be further from the truth. Steelhead aren't, in fact, exceedingly hard to take on a fly rod, or on any other kind of tackle, for that matter. The ease or difficulty by which steelhead are taken on rod and reel is directly proportionate to their numbers in the river. I was to learn this truth only on my trip to British Columbia.

Snowcapped glacial mountains rose on three sides of the river valley. That barrier to the west was the Bulkley Range, a mountainous division marking the end of British Columbia's interior plateau and the beginnings of B.C.'s dank coastal forests of Sitka spruce, Western hemlock, and rising Pacific mists. On this side of the Bulkleys, the land pretty much resembled the Rocky Mountain West, with alpine peaks, hay ranches, and forests of lodgepole, mixed conifer, and plenty of aspen. It sort of put me in mind of Montana. On the other side of the mountains, British Columbia would begin to look like Alaska.

I had come to one of the last pristine places on the North American continent to fish for steelhead in rivers that were as clean as the rain falling from the sky. Along a land rim that extends from Russia to Alaska and down into California, native steelhead swim in rivers flowing into the Pacific Ocean. I had come to British Columbia to find the last great run of steelhead left on my continent. These were more than just sport fish to me. In the Pacific Northwest, they stood for the last of the wild.

SUMMER RIVER, WINTER RIVER

I FIRST CAME TO THE North Umpqua River by way of the Oregon desert. The desert can come as a bit of a shock to someone who thinks that it does nothing but rain in the Pacific Northwest. Fully two-thirds of Oregon is a sagebrush desert steppe. It was August, and I felt like I was being slid into an oven. I was on a cross-country trip, driving from Montana to the Cascade Mountains, having just left Yellowstone Park behind me. Earlier that summer I had quit a good job where I lived back East just to take a year off so I could fly-fish for trout in the Rocky Mountain West. I had never fished for steelhead before, but it seemed like a good idea. Now I was looking for a river that flowed into the Pacific Ocean.

I drove to Bend, where the desert meets the high Cascades. Climbing west toward the plateau at Diamond Lake, I passed from a forest of skinny lodgepoles into much denser stands of Douglas fir. The desert air suddenly grew cool and refreshing. I climbed steadily into this fir forest and then began a descent down a shady, tree-lined corridor. Suddenly there was a spraying river next to me on the right. There it was, the North Umpqua River, racing swiftly through a canyon in dancing riffles and fast pocket water.

The North Umpqua had a forest reflection that was equal measures of Douglas fir and Oregon sky. It was a small and tumbling stream where it emerged below Soda Springs Dam. By the time it reached the campgrounds at Boulder Creek and Eagle Rock, the rushing pools had spread out and the runs were more clearly defined. I crossed over a bridge, the river now on my left, and looked at a shallow cobblestone flat sweeping around a bend that I would later learn was a spawning redd for chinook salmon. The river continued to flash through the trees below the highway's steep grade. Just above the Dry Creek Store, the North Umpqua dropped hundreds of feet below the highway, and it was a long, precipitous plunge off the embankment to the river. A mile below Dry Creek, the river swept away unseen around a long horseshoe-shaped bend, and when it came back into view the sight was every bit as dramatic as upstream, with the forest river frothing in rapids and plunging pools. In the mileage below Apple Creek, the North Umpqua continued to rush in whitewater chutes through dark basaltic rock shaded by immense stands of Douglas fir.

Four miles or so below Apple Creek, just around the corner from Island Campground, an old trestle known as the Mott Bridge crossed high above the river. Off to the right, Steamboat Creek came in, the largest tributary in the canyon. The North Umpqua doubled in width below Steamboat Creek. I didn't know it then, but I had come to a series of famed pools known as the Camp Water.

Upstream of Mott Bridge, Surveyor Pool lay in the shade of Douglas firs that were the size of mature redwood trees. The river poured over a bedrock of black volcanic basalt. Immediately below the Mott Bridge, in the eponymously named Bridge Pool, the river cut a deep channel between reefs of ledgerock. Well downstream the river passed in a smooth glide over two very jagged, sharp reefs known as Sawtooth. Just below Sawtooth, among streaming riffles, lay two small pools known as Hayden's Run and Sweetheart. A few yards below them was the Confluence Pool marking the spot where Steamboat Creek came into the Umpqua. And below this was the reefbound run known as the Station Pool, so named because a Forest Service station had once been set up directly across from the pool on the north bank. Because it was situated just below Steamboat Creek, a major spawning tributary, Station Pool was probably the most productive pool on the North Umpqua.

Below Station, the river fanned out into streaming riffles and a brief whitewater rapid. At the head of this rapid, a narrow chute tried to contain the currents of the upper Boat Hole. As the riffles and whitewater calmed down and played themselves out, the Boat Hole broadened into a wide flat of forest-green water bending around an expansive gravel bar, one of the few gravel bars on the river. It was a magnificent green pool, the largest pool on the Umpqua, a great convex mirror of sky and forest.

The water of the Boat Pool passed by like a bolt of cold green silk, and the river began to slide over a series of submerged reefs. These brown bedrock reefs formed the Kitchen Pool, so named because they had once been directly in line of sight of a kitchen tent in the first steelhead camp ever established on the river, the one set up by Major Lawrence Mott on the south bank, back in 1929. A steelhead lodge had later been built on the site of the old tent camp, but it was gone now, no trace remaining.

Below the tailout of the Kitchen Pool, the current passed into a narrow opening of ledgerock that formed a half-collar around a pool known as the Fighting Hole. Below this, and running for several hundred yards downstream, were three separate and distinct chambers of ledgerock known as the Upper, Middle, and Lower Mott Pools. From where the trees plunged down to the steep south bank, all the way out to the Mott Pools at midstream, the bottom bedrock of the river was a confusing labyrinth of rippled ledges, shallow channels, and uneven rock chutes.

The river passed into Glory Hole and the Gordon Pool, and as it rounded a bend, its volume rose noticeably. High on a bluff on the north bank, the Steamboat Inn perched above the river in the shade of massive sugar pines. On the opposite bank, even higher up on a foot trace on Maple Ridge, a hiker could gaze down through the trees at the roaring waterfalls beneath the inn and listen to its thunder filling the gorge. Around the bend and below the falling whitewater lay the last of the Camp Water pools: Upper and Lower Maple Run, Jeannie, Abernathy, Upper and Lower Takahashi, and Knouse.

I drove on past the Steamboat Inn, and through the screen of trees had a good look at pools that I would later come to know as the Ledges, the Tree Pool, Divide Pool, Williams Creek Riffle, Log Pool, Discovery Pool, Split Rock, Burnham,

Pulpit, Archie Creek, Coleman Creek, Cougar Creek, Bogus Creek, Rattlesnake, McDonald's Pool, Wright Creek, and Fairview. There were many more pools farther downstream, miles of them: Rip Rap, Fox Creek, Boundary, Susan Creek, the Honey Creek Riffles, Huckleberry, Baker Wayside, the Salmon Racks, and Famous Pool, to name some of the more prominent. There were parking pullouts alongside the road and scramble paths leading down to most of these pools and runs.

I found the North Umpqua uncommonly beautiful. A thick forest of Douglas fir shaded the canyon, cooling the summer breezes. The Douglas firs towered above the river and were as thick around as old-growth redwood. The river ran over ledges of black basaltic rock, and it made a beautiful music down among its boulders. The North Umpqua in its canyon had perfect pitch. Wild blackberries grew in abundance along the north bank, releasing their perfume into the forest-scented breeze.

I knew that the North Umpqua had a great tradition. I was aware that Jack Hemingway, the eldest son of the novelist Ernest Hemingway, had called the Camp Water, those pools directly below Steamboat Creek, "the greatest stretch of summer steelhead water in the United States." The famous fishing lodge on the river, the Steamboat Inn, was practically a shrine to steelhead fishing. The North Umpqua had been Zane Grey's favorite river. He had named the Ledge Pool, or the Ledges, and local fishermen had named the two Takahashi pools in honor of the author's Japanese field cook.

While it's good to stand and watch a river, it's always better to fish it. And so I pulled tackle and waders from the trunk of my car and rigged up. The North Umpqua was full of summer steelhead, and it seemed a crime not to try and catch one on my first day.

I found the rubble bottom and slippery bedrock ledges very tricky wading at first, and I fell in several times. I won't ramble on about the hours and days I spent trying to catch my first steelhead. Anyway, they say that steelhead are fish of a thousand casts.

For days steelhead flashed all around me. They leapt out of the water and shook themselves in the air. It unnerved me to see trout the size of salmon. There had been nothing like this in my fishing experience. All around me, fly-fishermen were catching steelhead and I wasn't; I would watch a struggling fish leaping crazily at the end of an angler's line, and I would turn into a manic-depressive.

Every morning I would come down to the river and go through the same motions. I knew the drill well. It became a ritual. Cast . . . strip . . . cast. One step downstream, and re- peat. A familiar rhythm set in, and my mind would begin to wander. I believe I was sitting in a bar in San Francisco having a beer when the steelhead grabbed my fly.

There's no mistaking the solid yank of a summer steelhead. It's quite different from the gentle tap of a trout. The strike came as a great surprise. It was as if the hand of Zeus had reached out of the river.

My rod bowed under an incredible weight. A great throbbing creature seemed to pass up the rod and into my arm. A steel- head shattered the pool's surface, splashing and spraying drop- lets of water all around. It jumped a second time, flashing silver in the sun, and ran twenty yards of line off my reel. How I managed to hold on to that wildly erupting fish I'll never know. I had never experienced anything like it in trout fishing. But after a fifteen-minute fight, I slid my catch over near the bank to admire her, an iridescent henfish still bright from an ocean that was more than a hundred miles distant. The steelhead's back was dark green and speckled like a trout's. Its shining sides were tinged by a vapor of rose that seemed to be awash in a silver luminescence. Within the pink cast on the shining armor was an almost invisible lavender mist that contributed to the general iridescence.

Imagine a tiny trout that is born in a mountain river backed by giant Douglas firs. The tiny smolt disappears into the blue Pacific and returns several years later as big and heavy and powerful as a salmon. This fish leaps waterfalls and swims up sunlit rapids to get back to this spot in the river, only to run afoul of a novice steelhead fisherman from New Jersey.

I am staring down in awe at my first-ever steelhead. Gratefully, and with the utmost reverence, I release the magnificent fish back into the river unharmed. And yet the North Umpqua will not willingly release me. I cannot even begin to calculate the damage that has been done. After such an afternoon, on such a gorgeous river, I am the one who has been caught.

One of the country's loneliest stretches of coastline begins somewhere north of San Francisco and extends all the way up through Oregon almost to Portland. Blue sea and white surf contrast with deep green forests and weathered gray barns. Here folks live in small coastal towns and rural hamlets, and their livelihoods depend on logging, fishing, farming, dairy ranching, sheep herding, and occasionally pot smuggling. America's best vintage wines are grown in vineyards inland. Along the fogbound coast, Victorian gingerbread homes and white New England fishing settlements sit atop ocean palisades. The forested coastal mountains are drained by a labyrinth of purling salmon and steelhead rivers. That part of the region lying in California has come to be known as the Redwood Empire.

Close by the Oregon border, California's Smith River meets the ocean amid the majesty of coastal redwoods. This is a steep and lonely region of cold summer fogs and winter rains. The Smith drains the Siskiyou Mountains, one of the few ranges in the western United States that runs from east to west. Like California's Coastal Range, the Siskiyous are entirely free of glacial ice. Somehow the advancing glaciers of the last ice age missed them. Rivers born in the Siskiyous, rivers like the Smith, and the Chetco, which is just over the border in Oregon, run with exceptional clarity where they have not been logged. The Smith River flows either emerald or jade depending on whether it has rained, and it is always the first river in northern California to drop and clear after a heavy storm.

I have driven six hours from my home in San Francisco to be on the Smith River. It has been five months since I caught my first steelhead in the North Umpqua. The Smith has become my winter steelhead river of choice. I discovered it shortly after moving to northern California. I was a trout fisherman gone wrong. I had given up my first love in order to pursue steelhead. I still loved trout; but steelhead filled me with wonder.

At Jedediah Smith State Park, I found myself looking at frothing creeks feeding into the Smith River from an unspoiled forest of Douglas fir, western hemlock, cedar, and old-growth redwood. Redwood National Park in California was created out of three existing state parks, Jedediah Smith being one. The Smith's magnificent redwood forest has never been logged. The Smith River itself has never been dammed. It is the only river of any consequence left in California not to have a dam on it. In autumn, the sylvan stream hosts vast runs of king salmon, and these are the largest king salmon seen in any river in California. In winter, California's biggest steelhead arrive, brutes weighing up to twenty-five pounds.

Everyone living up here seems to be either a fisherman, a logger, or a pot farmer. Or a prison guard. California's maximum-security penitentiary at Pelican Bay is close by. I stop at a wide spot in the road that comprises the entire hamlet of Hiouchi, which is just downstream of the forks of the Smith. There is a combined gas station–and–mini-mart, a rather mildewed motel, a bait shop, and a cafe. The mini-mart seems to be the town's cultural center. You can buy fried chicken, corn dogs, cold beer, beef jerky, and fishing tackle inside. Hanging on the walls are eye-popping mounts of steelhead and Chinook salmon of mind-boggling weight. Next to the door is a wall covered with Polaroid snapshots of fishermen who are standing next to their dead catches suspended from a rather fierce-looking grappling hook attached to a scale in front of the store. I don't see any photos of fly-fishermen releasing fish.

"Can anyone suggest a good spot on the river where I might be able to wade and fly-fish?" I ask the room. Everyone stares back at me as if I have just announced that I am to be in a performance of *Swan Lake*.

The Smith is ideal for bait casters, hardware fishermen, and terminal tackle-jockeys. It is the river of the slinky, the Spin-'n-Glo, and the lead pencil. It is a hard river to fly-fish. It is not a particularly easy river to wade. Its currents are deceptive and so strong they can sweep a fly out from under a steelhead before the fish even has a chance to see it. The Smith's winter-run steelhead are bottom huggers; unlike summer steelhead, steelhead in cold water will not travel far to chase a fly nor swim off the bottom to grab one that is fished anywhere near the surface. Heavy-grain shooting heads or sinking fly lines are the order of the day on the Smith, and these are not always pleasant to cast.

The steelhead in the Smith River are hard to hook; even harder to land. The river has three forks. All but a mile of the North Fork is closed for fishing. The Middle Fork of the Smith, the shortest branch, is a rather swift stream due to a rather steep gradient, and full of rapids. The current rarely has a chance to slow down and kayakers will do better in here than fly-fishermen. And yet interspersed throughout the fast runs and raging chutes are one or two shallow, gravel-bottom pools that end in slick tailouts, where a fly-fisherman can actually wade out into the river far enough to swing a wet fly through good holding water.

The South Fork is the hardest to reach and least-fished branch of the Smith River. Its deep canyon is also the wildest branch of the river. The good water is a long drop down from a narrow road that winds high above the river. The South Fork canyon's road is frequently closed by rockfalls and mudslides.

But there are sixteen miles of legal steelhead water in the canyon, and a few pools suited for a wading fly-fisherman.

Just above the town of Hiouchi, the Middle and South Forks join to form the main stem, Smith River, and it is in this lower mileage that the vast majority of salmon and steelhead are caught. In this stretch, the Smith is big and impressive and flanked by the tallest redwood spires. Driftboat traffic is intense and gear fishing all the rage. Many of the gravel-bank pools on the lower river are quite suitable for wading and fly-fishing. The only problem comes from driftboats floating over your line.

On my first day ever fishing the Smith River, a dozen driftboats ran over my line, and it seemed to me this was done on purpose. The driftboats were manned by professional fishing guides who were taking clients out on California's premier steelhead river. The main stem of the Smith had been overtaken by a go-getting commercial euphoria. When I protested to one of these guides after he floated over my water, he calmly informed me that his boat wouldn't spook the steelhead. This was like Nixon telling America he was not a crook.

On this bright January morning there are any number of good places where I can fish. I can go to the campground at Jedediah Smith Park and try the Park Hole under the redwoods. Or I can cross to the other side of the river and fish a good steelhead run known as the White Horse Riffle. I can try my luck at either the Bluff Hole or the Rain Gauge Riffle or the Cable Hole, which lies directly behind the Hiouchi Cafe. Or I can find a deserted gravel bar on the Middle Fork where I can swing a fly, or climb down into the South Fork's deep canyon. Either way I won't have to contend with driftboats. Or I can go below the Hiouchi Bridge to the Society Hole, a pool made famous in the salmon fishing stories of Russell Chatham.

The day is clear and almost windless. A California steelhead fisherman can't ask for anything better than green water and winter sunshine. My breath condenses in the frosty air. It is about ten degrees colder in the shade of the redwoods. I slip on a fleece pullover. Already encased in thermal underwear, I struggle into a pair of insulated neoprene waders. My feet are snug inside ski socks, and I pull a ski cap tightly over my ears. Feet and ears are the first to go in cold weather. If your head and feet get cold you won't last much more than a few hours on the river. I pull on a pair of fingerless woolen gloves. These water-resistant gloves will allow me to handle wet lines and flopping fish in an ice-cold river without going numb. I have learned the hard way that winter steelhead are caught only by fishermen who have learned how to stay warm and dry.

In the Pacific Northwest, steelhead fishing is a kind of religion, and winter fishing is strictly for its monks. You can stand for hours in freezing water, casting your heart out for a phantom that might not even be in the river or there in so few numbers as to make it hardly worth the effort. At least the steelhead faithful have their redwood churches to pray in.

I follow a footpath that leads through a forest of lacy ferns and massive redwood boles straining to touch heaven. Deeply filtered sunshine slants in shafts down into the forest. "Dim aisles in ancient cathedrals," wrote the poet T. S. Eliot, who never saw a redwood tree as far as I know. The redwoods are so tall they seem to link earth and sky. What little sunlight reaches the forest floor has begun as a green glow diffused in a canopy high overhead. It is like looking into light that has passed underwater. A silence seems to come out of the emerald moss that is growing on every fallen trunk and redwood log, out of the carpet of soft duff that covers the forest floor.

Redwoods get their name from the auburn color of the tree bark. This soft bark can grow as much as a foot thick on the oldest and tallest trees. This grove I am walking though is pure virgin redwood, the kind they call old-growth. Some of the oldest trees in Redwood National Park have trunks that boast more than two thousand annual rings. They are the tallest living things on earth, and they are also among the oldest, alive when Columbus set foot in the New World. And yet it can also be said that no tree in the ancient redwood forest can be more than thirty years old. Only a thin cambium layer beneath the bark of any tree is living tissue. The rest is dead wood. And yet a redwood tree seems every inch a living entity.

This is what is known as a temperate rain forest. The moist breath of the Pacific arrives as summer fog and winter rain, and the ocean releases her load of moisture onto these trees in the form of one hundred inches of precipitation a year. The redwoods even make their own rain. The forest literally breathes, the trees drawing up groundwater by the hundreds of gallons, from the roots to the crowns, releasing it into the air as condensation.

I pass fallen redwood trunks scattered throughout the forest, decaying by degrees into a moist carpet of duff, mosses, and ferns. Mushrooms and toadstools are growing on rotting logs or at the base of huge redwood burls and trunks. The giant redwoods in this grove are mixed with a few equally impressive

Douglas firs, and there is an understory to this forest made up of bigleaf and vine maple, huckleberry, salal, wood rose, azalea, and an abundance of rosebay rhododendron. The tallest redwoods are growing in groves closest to the stream flats. On the ridges and hillsides above these flats, the guardian groves are gradually giving way to a mixed forest of younger redwoods, tan oaks, and stunted chinquapin poking out of steep cliffs like bonsai shrubs in a Japanese garden.

I emerge from the forest and walk out onto a sunlit gravel bar beside the river. There are several other fishermen here. It hasn't rained in some time, so the river is the color of an emerald. Beside the bank, a bed of stones lies under clean water so transparent it is impossible to correctly judge the depth. Even in the shallows, the water is deeper than it at first appears. Like the virgin redwoods that rise above the banks, the Smith River is pristine and beautiful almost beyond comprehension.

At midstream, sunlight penetrates almost to the bottom of the river, highlighting the remarkable emerald tint. This distinctive aqua-green shine comes not only from the water's purity and the reflections of redwood trees all around but also from a mineral called serpentine that is found in the canyon bedrock. The emerald shade makes the river stones that are flickering on the bottom appear gold and green, depending on the depth, and in places the river pools so deeply that light is turned away two fathoms down in black-green holes. Olive boulders become dimly visible in mysterious underwater grottoes, and in the shallows the water is so light-stricken and transparent that I can actually see the shadows of steelhead over the pebbles.

Standing knee-deep in the river, backed by giant redwoods, an angler is drawing a steelhead toward the bank. The winter fish is like a fallen god. Its splendid body is pearlescent, with just the faintest hint of pink. This steelhead has been out of the ocean no more than a few days. Strong as ocean fish, smart as river trout, that's how fishermen describe steelhead. I admire the beached god, an animal to be worshiped.

The steelhead appears aerodynamic, shaped like a fuselage. Sleek and very strong looking, the steelhead's back is a shade between gunmetal-gray and metallic green with many trout speckles. Its flanks shine like stamped silver. In the zone of transition between the gunmetal and the silver sheen is a blush of lavender iridescence so faint as to be almost invisible. On the fish's side, and on the belly that is shining white like a pearl, there is a similarly faint cast of pink-and-lavender radiance.

The steelhead's unblinking eye is fixed on the sky and the redwoods. It is out of its element, drowning in air. It has no memory of the ocean's blue immensity nor of the birth river it has ascended. It cannot even know how it has struggled on the end of an angler's line. It doesn't even know that it is dying. It is only a collection of reflexes and a servant to its instincts. And yet it is one of the Pacific Northwest's true marvel animals.

The biological history of the Smith River can be said to be contained in this one steelhead. The fish has been swimming upstream carrying life like an Olympic torch. Its spawning ground is imprinted in its genes. The fish is a library of genetic knowledge about the river.

Like a salmon, a returning steelhead brings the fertility of the ocean up with it. Strictly speaking, a steelhead is not a salmon but a seagoing rainbow trout; yet they are so alike as to be practically the same fish. Smith River steelhead can grow larger than twenty-five pounds in this river; and the salmon fifty and sixty pounds.

The Smith is only one of hundreds of rivers pouring out of the coastal forests of the Pacific Northwest. Somewhere steelhead are ascending these rivers every month of the year in order to spawn, pushing upstream in silver squadrons. From northern California to the Canadian border, every river and stream drawn by gravity toward the Pacific will likely hold at least a few steelhead.

Think of the power of ocean-dwelling fish swimming upstream against a river current that never lets up. Now think of these fish steadily climbing toward mountains a thousand miles away. Pacific steelhead and salmon are capable of traversing three major Western mountain ranges: the gentle Coast Ranges that rise at the very edge of the continent and extend from California to Washington's Olympic Peninsula; the Cascades, which are a higher and more distant barrier; and the mile-high crests of the Rockies. Incredible as it seems, these ocean fish climb mountains. Some salmon and steelhead won't stop until they reach the Continental Divide. Idaho is a Rocky Mountain state and yet it legitimately can be considered part of the Pacific Northwest because there are steelhead and salmon in those rivers. If you need a definition of the Pacific Northwest, say it is wherever steelhead and salmon can swim to.

I wade into the river from the gravel bar. Although the pool is very smooth and clear, the current is very strong, and the water streams around my legs with such force that I can feel it trying to suck me toward the Pacific Ocean which is about ten or twelve miles distant. I wade out thigh-deep and cast as far as I can into the sliding emerald water. There is good holding water under the emerald shadows. I am certain steelhead will be out there. I fish the gravel bar from top to bottom but I get no strikes. I return to the head of the pool, tie on another, smaller fly, and proceed to do the whole thing all over again.

Halfway down the bar I feel a yank and suddenly I am attached to a large steelhead. I don't know which is fighting me harder, the river or the fish. I feel an incredible weight that is both steelhead and current. The steelhead hunkers for a moment on the bottom, and by following the trail of my slanting fly line I can see the steelhead at the other end of it writhing in the emerald depths. And then the fish flashes toward the surface and water explodes around him. The steelhead shoots downstream and is pulling me with him. I am still fighting both fish and current. I hold my rod high, running and splashing over the cobblestones, almost tripping and falling, the line singing off my reel. The fish is deep into the backing now; the line is coming off at an alarming rate. I hold tight and manage to slow the steelhead's run. Again the silver fish rises to the surface and the water boils. I pump, reeling tight, but the line starts unwinding again. I stumble over more stones to keep up with the departing fish. Twice I almost trip and fall. I certainly don't want to take a spill into this freezing water. Once again, I manage to check the steelhead's run. In the ensuing tug-of-war, I almost manage to turn the fish. Then the hook pulls free.

I sit down on the bank, shaken. No experience in fifteen

years of trout fishing has prepared me for anything like that. I look out over the redwood spires and see a golden eagle turning above the forest. The clear sound of the bubbling river is in my ears. I never want to leave this place.

CALIFORNIA DREAMING

THE PAINTER RUSSELL CHATHAM once wrote a story about California's finest salmon and steelhead river. He titled it "Wading for Godot." It was about how hard it was to catch salmon on the Smith River. The story contained a much larger metaphor about fishing in California: more and more the scene was resembling something out of the Theater of the Absurd.

I can't count the number of hours I spent standing waist-deep in California's green rivers trying to catch winter steelhead. I was so happy that at first I hardly noticed the raw and unfinished look of so many California streams. I felt so privileged to be fishing for something as wonderful as steelhead that I was barely aware I wasn't catching any. I thought that's the way things were supposed to be. A steelhead was a fish of a thousand casts, or so I had been told. I caught so few steelhead, I thought I had a Zen thing going on.

There is a small redwood stream a hundred miles north of San Francisco called the Gualala River. It is a very lovely winter steelhead river flowing through a redwood canyon. It is perhaps too popular, or at any rate, too close to the San Francisco Bay

Area. On weekends in January and February there can be as many as fifteen or twenty fishermen to a pool, the lineup shoulder-to-shoulder. Bait casters on one side of the river, fly-fishermen on the other, all glowering at one another. On week-days the scene wouldn't be quite so bad. I learned to fish the Gualala in the in-between moments, on those March and April days when only smaller bluebacks were running, and hookups and anglers were fewer and far between. Naturally I didn't catch many fish. This only reinforced my impression that steelhead were difficult to take on a fly rod.

One March morning, I found myself driving up to the Gualala River with my friend Andy Kubersky. As a teenager, Andy had played the French horn in the American Symphony Orchestra. Leopold Stokowski once threw a baton at his head. The temperamental conductor missed. An inner-ear condition, affecting Andy's balance, ended his chances of an orchestral career. Over time Andy exchanged the French horn for kitchen utensils, camera, and fly rod, which went some way toward satisfying his creative urges.

I asked Andy what he liked best about the Gualala River, and he told me it was the couch-shaped log under the redwoods where he took streamside naps. I think he goes fishing just to nap. "I hope to die, not in my sleep, but while napping," Andy once told me. He maintains there is a difference.

Andy told me he liked to stretch out, close his eyes, and fall asleep to the sound of falling water. What he disliked most about the Gualala River were the crowds. And the general scene. People telling him he was using the wrong fly line, or fishing in the wrong place, or not getting his fly down deep

27

enough. "People telling me I have to use a bonefish line if I hope to catch anything," Andy said. "As if fly-fishermen weren't catching steelhead on the Gualala for thirty years before anybody ever heard of bonefish lines."

One of the things that I most enjoyed about the Gualala River was the drive up the coast. Andy and I were treated to breathtaking views of the California headlands dropping into the Pacific. This wasn't exactly Big Sur, but it was a close second. We passed by Fort Ross, built on cypress cliffs high above the Pacific. Sheep grazed in meadow ranches that were hundreds of feet above the plunging surf. The Gualala, a very short river by steelhead standards, rises in Sonoma County's coastal mountains, part of the Coastal Range, and empties into the Pacific at the little town of Gualala.

We parked on a road along the south bank at the Sonoma County Campground and hiked through a redwood grove that led down to Miner Hole. An emerald carpet of redwood sorrel covered the ground, and bay laurel added its spiciness to the general forest fragrance. I could hear a low cannonade of surf about a mile distant.

Typical of California's shorter coastal rivers emptying directly into the Pacific, the Gualala began with a tide pool at the beach that ran parallel to the ocean before cutting through a sandbar at the mouth. Its sandy lagoon was bordered by cypress cliffs. Starting at the highway bridge at the head of the redwood canyon, and proceeding upstream for about two miles, were a number of clearly defined river pools that on this morning were vegetable-green. These pools, about eight of them, were the prime fly-fishing spots on the river. Each bend in the redwood canyon held a curving bar of sand and gravel on one side, and a deep green pool bulging against a steep bank of rocks and high forest on the other. The Gualala ran nowhere near as clear as the Smith. It rarely got that emerald look, on account of so much logging in the nearby hills. Yet the river was quite beautiful.

Steelhead need to make a transition from salt to fresh water before coming into a river to spawn. Once acclimated to the brackish water of a lagoon, steelhead are able to ascend into the lower pools of a river. They will rest for a few hours or several days in pools that rise and fall slightly with the tide. How long the steelhead would stay in those pools differed from river to river and even among fish of the same run. Miner Hole was one such tidal pool. When it rained, Gualala steelhead would swim out of Miner Hole and the lower river pools and move up either into the North Fork or farther up the main stem, both of which were very narrow mountain streams.

Miner Hole has a wide sandbar that is very popular with fly-fishermen, especially at its lower end, and several of these fellows had waded out from the sandbar and were firing shooting heads at the far bank. I don't particularly care for heavily weighted shooting heads, as I find them almost impossible to mend, and I have trouble controlling their drifts in slow currents such as these. The truth is, I am not a very good caster.

Not wanting to crowd Miner Hole, Andy and I walked a considerable distance up the bar, where it came round a bend, and crossed the shallows to the other side of the river so we could fish Thompson Hole from the north bank. I left the pool's tailout for Andy to fish. I began to fish the run that lies just above the head of the pool, where the current sweeps past a fallen tree half submerged in the river. I was using a streamer fly known as a Green Butt Skunk, a rather common steelhead pattern. Right above the head of the pool, in water that was only a foot deep, a steelhead seized my fly, and the hard yank jolted me out of a reverie.

The reel squawked like an angry duck as the steelhead took off downstream. I tightened up on the line and checked the steelhead's flight. Though it was a small fish, its fight seemed to come out of some deep panic. My rod dipped up and down spasmodically as the steelhead fought for all it was worth. I had it over on the bank in minutes, only to have it flop around, jump back in the river, and take off again. I beached the fish one more time. Now that I had a chance to examine it more closely, I could see the steelhead weighed no more than four pounds. It was skinny and starved. It was a kelt, a winter steelhead that had already spawned, and was now on its way back to the sea. Unlike Pacific salmon, which die immediately after spawning, some steelhead survive. Steelhead have no need to eat when they come into a river to spawn. Their primary concern is the marriage bed awaiting them in the gravel upstream. I estimated that my steelhead, a cockfish, would have weighed around six pounds when he first arrived from the ocean. He had lost fully two pounds of his fighting weight. A woman had been his downfall—it's the same old story everywhere. But emaciated and weakened as he was, this fish had put up a real scrap. I have caught four-pound resident rainbow trout in Montana that didn't fight half as hard as this starved searun fish. That was the difference between ocean fish and river fish.

I looked around for my friend, wanting to let him know I had caught a "six-pound" steelhead. But Andy was taking a nap, curled up against his favorite redwood log.

That was a good day on the Gualala River. I have had less idyllic times on that stream. I have been on the river when squads of Bay Area fly-fishermen were assaulting it like urban guerrillas from the Symbionese Liberation Army. I have seen wholesale pool-hogging, where fishermen played strictly by California Rules, the first rule being that there were none. I will never again make the mistake of fishing the Gualala River on a weekend. Even on weekdays, when word got out that the steelhead were in, the Gualala would become way too crowded to suit my tastes.

The problem with the Gualala River was that, remote as it seemed, it was still too close to San Francisco. That was also the problem with the Russian River. The Russian is a long river flowing through lush vineyard and redwood country just north of San Francisco. Fog hangs in its valleys, and in winter the fern-covered earth in the few remaining redwood groves becomes fragrant with the perfume of damp mulch. In its final mileage, the Russian empties into the sea at Jenner amid rolling coastal hills and spacious dairy and sheep ranches. There was a time on the Russian River when runs of over thirty thousand wild winter steelhead would come in from the ocean. It was possible then for a fly-fisherman such as the legendary Bill Schaadt, fishing a single season on the Russian River from November through February, to hook and land as many as eight hundred steelhead.

I fished on the Russian River many times. It had been raped and pillaged by its citizens. Dams, viniculture, gravel mining, and the metastasis of suburban sprawl moving up from the Bay Area had ruined it completely. In order to get in any decent fishing, I would have to make a longer drive north to the Eel, the Klamath, and the Trinity.

Sometimes I would go up to the Klamath River in early autumn to fish the run of steelhead known as half-pounders. The Klamath is the second-longest river in California, flowing out of a rather forlorn yet beautiful region of northern California, a landscape of forests and Indian reservations. Fog rises like a specter off the mountains, and Pacific fronts bring rain starting in autumn. The Klamath River runs the color of forest tannins and the bronze rocks lying in its streambed appear dark in the tea-stained river. Salmon and steelhead start coming into the lower river in July, but the Klamath is really known for its autumn run of half-pounders.

On the West Coast, sexually immature fish that return after less than a year in the ocean are called "half-pounders." The name is a bit misleading, as these steelhead can weigh anywhere between one and five pounds and still be called "half-pounders." On Atlantic salmon streams, their equivalent would be grilse, salmon that have come home after only a year at sea. Grilse can weigh up to nine pounds. Atlantic salmon anglers have a saying that if you have only caught a grilse, you can't say you've caught a salmon. West Coast steelhead fishermen are more broad-minded than that. They are willing to call the trout they catch "steelhead." And that's what these Klamath fish were to me—trout. Big trout, yes, but still trout. The junior steelhead I caught on the Klamath averaged three and four pounds. The only sporting way to catch one was with a light trout rod. It didn't feel at all like steelhead fishing to me, more like trout fishing. One could think of the Klamath's half-pounders as California's largest trout or its smallest steelhead. Being a pessimist, I chose to view this particular glass as half empty.

True, larger steelhead could sometimes be found in the Klamath, bound for the forks of the Trinity, Salmon, and Scott Rivers. They might hold in large, deep pools that formed on the main river directly below the mouths of these tributaries; and it was always a terrific surprise to catch a big Klamath steelhead on a puny trout rod. But that's the advantage of being a pessimist. Optimists, always expecting the best, are only setting themselves up for disappointment; whereas pessimists, expecting the worst, more often than not are pleasantly surprised.

Sometimes I would head into the turkey-vulture canyons of the Trinity River. The Trinity country had a godforsaken look. People said Sasquatches lived up here. The Trinity Mountains weren't popular with hikers the way the Sierra was popular, not scenic the way Yosemite was. But the canyon of the Trinity was deep, and driving along the highway I could catch glimpses of jade-green pools below.

The conifer forest had a bluish tint that was different from the redwood coast's rain-forest lushness. In the hazy distances, I could see hydraulic mining spoils and old clear-cuts. The Trinity River was boulder-studded, with steep forests and rock walls closing in. The river lay mostly in shadow, but light emanated as much from the river as from the sky. At the junction of Willow Creek, Route 299 left the river to continue westward all the way to Eureka on a series of wildly descending hairpins ending at the Pacific coast.

Willow Creek was a good place for legends. The crossroads town billed itself as "Sasquatch City, the Bigfoot Capital of California." Willow Creek looked like a Tom Robbins roadside attraction, with cheesy curio shops, Bigfoot totem poles, tourist museums, and even a Bigfoot golf course.

Bigfoot hunters had taken plaster casts of giant footprints found around the banks of Willow Creek. And it was very near this spot, in 1967, close by the Hoopa Indian Reservation, that the most famous Bigfoot sighting of all occurred. A Bigfoot hunter named Roger Patterson caught the apeman on film. A Sasquatch buff, Patterson had earlier authored a flamboyant paperback entitled, *Do Abominable Snowmen of North America Really Exist?* He seemed to think the answer was yes. It was difficult to tell if the creature he caught on film was the mysterious giant of Pacific Northwest Indian mythology or a man in a cheap monkey suit.

The philosopher Sallust said that myths are things that never happened but are always true. In much of the Pacific Northwest, Indian myth has been turned into kitsch. Both Indian folklore and modern eyewitness testimony support the theory of a giant Pacific Northwest primate. In theory, Bigfoot descends from a great ape, perhaps *Gigantopithicus*, whose fossil remains, dating back to the Pliocene and Pleistocene eras, have been unearthed in Asia. This giant primate, which might have been Tibet's legendary yeti or Abominable Snowman, may have once crossed the land bridge that existed between Siberia and Alaska, migrating southward, and continued to survive as a relic species in the mountainous and heavily forested regions of the Pacific Northwest. Its range is said to extend all the way from northern California to British Columbia. The only problem with this theory is the complete absence of any fossil record for such a creature ever having lived in North America. Despite thousands of "sightings," not a single fossil or bone has ever been recovered.

In California, citizens actually petitioned the state government in Sacramento to pass laws that would officially list Bigfoot as a protected species, proposing criminal penalties for killing one. Meanwhile, no one seemed to be asking for similar protections for the salmon and steelhead in the Trinity River, creatures fast becoming as scarce as Bigfoot—but with the disadvantage of being real. The summer run of steelhead on the Trinity was obliterated after much of the river was diverted for California's agricultural miracle, the Central Valley Project, back in the sixties. The Trinity hasn't been the same since.

I drove to the town of Weitchpec that sits on a bluff overlooking the junction of the Trinity and Klamath Rivers. There is a seven-mile gorge in the lower river. Five miles south of Weitchpec, a poorly marked trail leads down to the Cabin Riffle, perhaps the finest fly-fishing water on the Trinity.

When I got to the bottom of the trail, I found myself facing three-quarters of a mile of ideal steelhead holding water. I cast into the riffles and concentrated on the fly fluttering down into the primary holding water. Twice I got light tugs, but I couldn't tell if they were from steelhead. A lid of canyon shadow began to cover the river.

In one drift my fly stopped suddenly. I felt a sharp tug, and when I pulled up, a bright steelhead lifted from the pool in an acrobatic leap. Water boiled as the steelhead attempted to shake the fly that was firmly implanted in its jaw. It leapt three more times, and then escorted me down the riffle. I fought to regain line. Ten minutes later, I was beaching a flopping seven-pound buck.

The steelhead had a dull red stripe along its fading chain mail. Steelhead change color after entering a river, their skin cells darkening according to sexual urges. A fish taken immediately from the water has a kind of transitory resplendence. This resplendence fades if the fish is killed or left out of the water for very long.

I returned the steelhead to the stream, thinking of the do-gooders who wanted Bigfoot to be listed as an endangered species, like protecting unicorns. I didn't believe in Bigfoot, but I did believe in its habitat. I could understand how the Pacific Northwest had given birth to a story of an American Grendel. It seemed to be a place where it was not inconceivable a Sasquatch might roam around unseen. But the very wilderness that had given birth to the mythology of Bigfoot was disappearing fast, and with it the creatures that dwelt in Bigfoot's world. Now people were fighting over the remnants, over spotted owls and logging roads. When the wilderness was finally tamed and gone, and the last steelhead had vanished up the Trinity River, who would believe that giants had ever walked this land?

Sometimes I would drive north to fish the Eel River, one of California's longest steelhead rivers, and once the southern-most range for summer steelhead in the United States. Russell Chatham described the Eel as once having been "the greatest salmon and steelhead river in the world." Like the Trinity, the Eel had lost its summer run. The headwaters of the Eel River had been logged mercilessly, taking away the forest cover and the shade. The river couldn't stay cool enough in summer to shelter fish. A few summer fish still straggled into the Middle Fork of the Eel, but this was a vestigial run only. In addition to its logging scars in the headwaters, the river also had been wounded by the construction of the Potter Valley Dam upstream. Once the Eel was the paramount steelhead river in California; today fly-fishermen have largely given it up as a lost cause.

When I first came to California, I used to fish the Eel because it still had a decent, although much diminished, run of winter steelhead. It was not unusual for me to have a pool all to myself. Most serious fly-fishermen were elsewhere, crowding out rivers like the Smith.

I preferred the South Fork of the Eel to its main stem. The southern branch drained sixty miles of redwood canyons. Along the Avenue of the Giants, groves of virgin old-growth shaded the riverbanks. These giant trees were part of Redwood National Park. The coastal redwood, *Sequoia sempervirens*, grew only along a narrow strip of land bounded by the Pacific Ocean and the Coast Range, a habitat extending only five hundred miles, from Big Sur to just over the Oregon border. Redwoods depend on warm, moist ocean air. And depending on how far the ocean's fog penetrated, these great redwood forests extended anywhere from five to twenty miles inland. Redwoods once blanketed two million acres of California. Today only five percent of that precious old-growth remains. Half the old-growth trees are in private forests subject to logging. The remainder are preserved inside a handful of nature theme parks, like Muir Woods, near San Francisco, or Redwood National Park, a forty-six-mile strip of parkland along the northern coast. Most redwood groves standing today in California are second- and third-growth forests.

All steelhead on the South Fork of the Eel River are wild. That's the good news. Hatchery fish turn up the main stem of the Eel at a place called The Forks. South Fork steelhead have never seen the inside of a hatchery; they are all streamborn, wild fish. When I went up to the South Fork, I would fish in emerald pools reflecting redwood spires, and hardly ever see another fly-fisherman.

I never caught an Eel River steelhead. Like so many other California fly-fishermen, I, too, gave up on the Eel. And my experience there only reinforced my belief that steelhead presented some kind of ultimate challenge, as they say in the sporting press.

The romance of fishing in California was beginning to wane for me. I was starting to see California's rivers for what they really were. Steelhead fishing on the Klamath was really trout fishing. The Eel, once the greatest steelhead river in California, was a ghost river. The Smith, a flawless river in every other respect, was overrun by my fellow anglers and a flotilla of driftboats.

Little of this seemed to matter, anyway, as it would rain so hard throughout the winters in northern California that there never seemed to be any opportunity to go fishing; California's steelhead fishery was largely a winter proposition. Historically speaking, that wasn't always the case. Thanks to logging and dams, California's summer runs of steelhead are mostly extinct. In fact only a fraction of California's original number of steelhead remains at all—and these are predominantly winter fish. All but the largest of California's coastal rivers are blocked at the ocean by sandbars, and steelhead can't pass up through them until winter storms break them open. This explains the nature of California's winter steelhead fishery. Winter fishing is for those whose tastes run toward asceticism. Fishing in the cold and rain isn't exactly pleasant, and the heavy lines and the rods required to land winter steelhead would make a trout purist faint.

I would spend most of steelhead season listening to rain drumming on the roof of my San Francisco apartment. By late November and December, Pacific storms would be battering the coast, the sandbars finally breaking open, allowing steelhead to swim into the shorter coastal streams. These winter rains made fishing both possible and impossible. There was a pattern to the winter storms. A series of low fronts would come in over the Pacific and it would rain for three or four days, and then the skies would clear for a short time. This lull was followed by the next storm. But during the lulls the rivers would remain discolored and wholly unsuitable for fly-fishing. Logging had destabilized the watersheds to the point that, with the trees and root systems gone, there was little left to hold soil in place when it rained. Just as the rivers started clearing and coming back into shape, it would rain all over again. This cruel pattern repeated itself all winter long. Unless there was a drought—and then things really turned bad. Many steelhead rivers had to be closed to fishing on account of low water flows.

Too many California rivers had that ravaged, unfinished look that came from logging. But forest clear-cutting wasn't the only problem. California's longest river, the Sacramento, once home to five species of salmon, now hosted only a few steelhead and a feeble run of king salmon kept alive by hatchery production. Dams blocked the upstream migration of anadromous fish into nearly every stream in the Sierra Nevada Mountains. The demise of the steelhead runs in the Central Valley, just as with those rivers along the coast, could be blamed on the usual suspects: dam construction cutting off historic spawning and nursery sites and altering stream flows; channelization and diversion of water for agricultural and urban use; and the discharge of sediment into watersheds from logging, road building, and real-estate development. There was only one pristine steelhead river remaining in California, and that was the Smith.

THE DOOMSDAY BOOK

AS A CALIFORNIA STEELHEAD fisherman I had come to realize that the smartest thing I could do was buy an Oregon fishing license. Whenever I started feeling sorry for myself, I would remember that I lived within a day's drive to the finest summer steelhead river in the United States. The North Umpqua was only an eight-hour drive from my home. If I left San Francisco in the early morning, I could be fishing the famous Camp Water by midafternoon. I would pitch a tent in the shade of Douglas firs and sugar pines and stay for weeks at a time.

I began to plan my fishing year around the North Umpqua. I would divide my time equally between California's redwood streams in wintertime, and the North Umpqua in summer and fall. I'd try to arrange it so I could spend at least one week each month, from July through October, fishing the North Umpqua. I wasn't always able to keep this schedule; but I came awfully close.

Given the opportunity, and the choice, I'd sooner fish for summer-run rather than winter steelhead. The solid yank from a summer steelhead was quite different from the tentative pull you'd get from a winter fish. Lower water temperatures in winter tended to slow down a steelhead's metabolism. Winter steelhead wouldn't move very far to take a fly; you'd have to bring the fly down to them. That usually meant fishing with a sink tip, or a full sinking fly line. And sinking lines weren't all that pleasurable to cast or mend. This kind of fishing tended to separate the men from the boys.

Summer steelhead were a much different story. They could be taken on floating lines and even on dry flies, which, being easiest, was my favorite way to fish for them. Summer fish usually ascended larger, longer river systems, like the North Umpqua. They came into the river early because they had to swim a long way to reach their spawning grounds. Although they stayed in fresh water for many months before spawning, they remained very bright, lively, and aggressive. A summer steelhead would move off the bottom and attack a streamer with something that in a human being would be considered enthusiasm. Summer fish made more earnest combatants. Those summer steelhead I caught on the North Umpqua River more than a hundred miles from the sea, jumped more, battled harder, and generally put up a bigger struggle than Gualala River steelhead of the same weight that were hooked just a day or two out of the ocean. (Smith River winter steelhead were almost impossible to land, but they were larger and took advantage of the Smith's stronger currents.)

The North Umpqua has a reputation for being something of a graduate school for fly-fishermen. Wading was difficult and frequently hazardous. Rocks on the stream bottom were very slick and the currents strong. Banks were heavily wooded, and in many cases difficult to make a backcast. North Umpqua steelhead were notoriously moody, even fickle. They saw a lot of anglers in a season. In midsummer, in very warm weather, the fish tended to stay very near the bottom, refusing to rise to the surface to chase flies. At those times it was difficult for a fly-fisherman to tease one up to the surface. If you were good enough to catch steelhead on the North Umpqua, you were ready to catch them anywhere.

The Umpqua River flows more than a hundred miles toward the ocean, but it is in its upper canyon on the North Fork that it has achieved fame as a fly-fishing river. Thirty-one miles of the canyon has been set aside for angling exclusively with a fly. The result is fly-fishing Nirvana.

The more I fished the North Umpqua, the more I began to notice the rivalry there among fly-fishermen. More and more, anglers were resorting to fishing with the aid of fluorescent strike indicators attached to long monofilament leaders. When the river was set aside for fly-fishing back in the 1950s, a further restriction had been included prohibiting anyone from attaching additional weight to a fly or line. This restriction was added to provide North Umpqua steelhead with a sanctuary in deeper water.

Californians, who had once pioneered shooting heads and lead-core sinking lines in order to get their flies down deep for winter steelhead, had advanced a new technique for catching the dour summer steelhead on the North Umpqua. By dread-drifting a heavily weighted nymph under a big fluorescent strike indicator—which acted much the same as a bobber in bait fishing—fly-fishermen using floating lines could get tremendously long drifts while taking weighted flies directly down to the steel-head on the bottom at the ends of their long monofilament leaders. Because the strike indicator acted like a hinge from which the bait hung, the fishermen could get much longer and deeper drifts than anything that could be achieved using a sink-ing or sink-tip line. Resting steelhead that didn't seem inclined to move very far and attack a streamer fly that was fished teas-ingly in the surface currents, in a traditional manner, were very susceptible to these deeply drifted baits, especially when they were passed directly in front of the fish's mouth. There was some question as to whether this was even fly-fishing. The strike-indicator boys seemed to be outfishing traditional fly-fishermen by about five to one. Traditionalists cried foul.

I spoke one time to Frank Moore about the controversy. Frank is the former owner of the Steamboat Inn and he once served as an Oregon commissioner of fish and game. He just might know more about the North Umpqua than any fisherman alive; he has been fishing it since the 1940s. Frank told me that strike-indicator fishing defeated the very purpose of the fly-only restriction. He feared it had contributed to steelhead mortality rates. In midsummer, with lots of angling pressure on the river, steelhead needed to be rested in order to recover. Often a single fish might be hooked several times a day by fishermen passing weighted flies under strike indicators. It wasn't always certain that a steelhead could survive being caught and released so many times within such a short period.

The strike-indicator fishermen I talked to didn't seem to think they were doing anything harmful, and suspected their rivals might be just a little jealous. I didn't know who was right and I wasn't sure I cared. Arguments between fishermen are like feuds between college academics, bitter only because the stakes are so small. I thought I was listening to some argument over transubstantiation of the Eucharist.

But the longer I thought about it, the more convinced I was that Moore and the other traditionalists held the moral high ground with their conservation argument. I tried fishing with a strike indicator several times myself and I didn't quite like the way it felt. I found it unpleasant to cast not only the weighted fly, but also the foam indicator, which was highly air-resistant. It didn't have the pleasing rhythm of regular fly-casting. I enjoyed traditional fly-fishing too much to give it up solely to increase the number of steelhead I caught. In fact, I couldn't imagine why anyone didn't want to fish with a dry fly on the North Umpqua, as I did.

If I had only one river to fish for the rest of my life, I suppose I would choose the North Umpqua. There was something about the dense mantle of Douglas fir that shaded the banks, something about the way the river cut through the dark bedrock. It was the most beautiful River I had ever seen. The pools offered many different kinds of challenges for a fly-fisherman. Each pool had its own distinct personality and character. Around each tree-lined bend lay ledge pools or cobblestone runs all suited to different methods of fly-fishing. I could spend all day on the slab-rock ledge pools of the Camp Water; or explore narrow whitewater rapids upstream; or work a fly through wide, classically contoured pools ending in smooth, gliding tailouts—and never exhaust the possibilities. There was a pool to suit every mood.

But the North Umpqua wasn't without its problems. Back in the 1950s, a dam had been constructed upstream and a highway built along the river grade. The number of summer fish always seemed to be either rising or falling according to some obscure stream voodoo. For example, when I first visited the river, in August of 1988, an incredible run of more than fifteen thousand summer steelhead came into the river. Only three years later, during a period of drought, fewer than five thousand summer steelhead were counted coming into the canyon water of the North Umpqua. The next year the run was even lower. Runs of wild summer steelhead on the North Umpqua have to be supplemented by hatchery fish, have been for a long time. (North Umpqua winter steelhead, a run averaging around eight thousand fish, are entirely wild.) Thanks to the presence of hatchery fish in the river, and their ability to spawn in the wild, over the years the average weight of a North Umpqua summer steelhead has gradually increased from seven to ten pounds, a silver lining in an otherwise dark cloud.

Most North Umpqua steelhead spawn in Steamboat Creek and Canton Creek, which are closed to fishing. I have seen as many as fifty steelhead resting in a single pool in those creeks. They are a favorite target of poachers, who kill the steelhead with dynamite.

Wherever one travels in steelhead country these days, for every fly in the water you will find a fly in the ointment. It might sound ungrateful for someone like myself to complain, when I have the opportunity to fish a redwood cathedral like the Smith in the winter, and the North Umpqua in the summer. Few people in life are given such choices. But increasingly what I found in steelhead country was leaving me disheartened.

I won't try to rush through the history of all that has gone wrong with the Pacific Northwest salmon and steelhead fishery. The American West Coast steelhead story is a long and complicated one, filled with tragic judgments and missed opportunities, and I can't even begin to convey the magnitude of all that went wrong. The story can't be crammed into a few paragraphs, and to give a full account would require another kind of book from the one I am writing. But it's important for readers to know something about what happened.

I have said that the Pacific Northwest is wherever steelhead and salmon can swim to. That is why Idaho, a Rocky Mountain state, can legitimately be considered a part of the Pacific Northwest. Salmon and steelhead can climb waterfalls and surmount the Cascade and Rocky Mountains, but they can't swim over dams. All of Idaho's native salmon and steelhead are either extinct or in danger of becoming extinct. This is due to eight dams that have plugged up the main stem of the Columbia River and the lower Snake River. Snake River coho salmon were declared extinct in 1986. Sockeye and chinook salmon are on the verge of extinction on the Snake. I can't remember the last time anyone caught a salmon in Idaho's Salmon River. Even with fish ladders to aid upstream migration, the dams on the Columbia and Snake have blocked the downstream migration of smolts to the ocean. Prior to those dams, the Columbia and Snake had formed the greatest steelhead and salmon passage in the world. The dams transformed the

Columbia into a chain of still-water impoundments. Without a moving current, a river can't flow. It is no longer even a river. Today salmon smolts have to be transported downstream by barge just so they can get to the Pacific Ocean. It's a little like witnessing the end of nature. If salmon could suffer indignity, imagine what theirs would be like.

The number of wild steelhead returning to the sagebrush basins of Idaho and the desert steppes of eastern Oregon and Washington has plunged from annual returns of sixty thousand fish to only eight thousand steelhead in recent years. (The higher figure was based on intermittent counts taken during the 1960s, when the runs were even then well below their historic numbers.) Of those returning steelhead, 95 percent are so-called A-run fish, steelhead that have spent one to two years at sea, and normally grow four to eight pounds in weight. Almost vanished are the B-run fish, steelhead that remain in the ocean from between two and four years, and average ten to fifteen pounds, with a few outstanding specimens weighing more than twenty pounds. Dworshak Dam on the North Fork of Idaho's Clearwater River, a tributary of the Snake, permanently blocked the upstream migration of what were once believed to have been America's largest steelhead, a genetic strain unique to that fork.

The number of healthy steelhead streams in the United States outside of Alaska can probably be counted on one hand's fingers. Only the steelhead rivers in the Olympic Peninsula, and a few that flow into Puget Sound, remain in relatively healthy shape today. In every other river in the U.S. Pacific Northwest south of Alaska, the steelhead have been proposed as candidates for some kind of listing under the Endangered Species Act.

In my own personal inventory of steelhead rivers, I can find only four or five truly prime streams left in the Lower Forty-eight. I'm talking about the kind of river where the landscape is still relatively intact, where an angler might be able to experience something a little like what fishermen had in the past. I mean rivers where one can still find something of the original, vanishing Northwest.

I would count the North Umpqua River as one such stream, because it is still the prettiest summer steelhead river in the United States. And I'd include the Skagit River against its magnificent backdrop of blue glacial mountains in Washington State, when wild spring steelhead are running in March and April. And I'd certainly include a few of those forest rivers flowing through the primeval old-growth of the Olympic Peninsula in early spring. There you have it: the best steelhead fishing in the United States outside of Alaska reduced to North Umpqua summer fish and big wild spring natives of the Skagit Valley and Olympic Peninsula. I realize that each of my choices reflects a compromise. The North Umpqua is bordered by a paved road along its magnificent canyon stretch, is dammed in its upper river, and has to rely on hatcheries to sustain its runs of wild steelhead. Anglers can go for days without touching a steelhead in the forests of the Olympic Peninsula, which are threatened by logging outside the protection of the national park. Sadly, the Skagit's days may also be numbered. The previous spring, the best guide on the river, Dec Hogan, went more than twenty days in prime time without a fish.

Every river, stream, and creek emptying into the Pacific, from northern California to the Canadian border, once had salmon and steelhead in them in healthy numbers. They swam everywhere there was running water. No longer. The story is much the same for salmonids and searun fish all over the world.

For example, there is no longer any quality Atlantic salmon fishing in our New England states. Dam construction and factory pollution have seen to that. Early in the century, Maine plugged up every single one of its formerly splendid salmon rivers for hydro power, blocking upstream migration to spawning grounds. Native brook trout and landlocked salmon are all that remain of Maine's prime cold-water game fishery. Efforts to restore historic June and July salmon runs in Maine seem more pitiable than anything else, the substitution of a pathetic simulacrum for what once existed in nature.

Atlantic salmon have suffered catastrophic declines in recent years—from more than a million mature salmon wintering off Greenland in the 1970s, to fewer than a hundred thousand now. Strong evidence points to a dramatically shrinking hospitable habitat in the North Atlantic, with the waters getting colder in late winter and early spring, and the salmon disappearing.

Some of the world's finest Atlantic salmon fishing is still found over the Maine border in Canada's Atlantic Maritime Provinces. Hard Maritime winters are followed by short, cool summers that create ideal conditions for salmon fishing among the beautiful birch forests of the North. But the privilege of fishing for Atlantic salmon is one you have to pay dearly for, as this is a sport fishery managed for the wealthy and influential.

New Brunswick has some of the best-known salmon fishing on the continent, but while the rivers are legally public waters, streambanks and fishing rights might be owned or leased by individuals, clubs, or outfitters. Salmon fishermen who live outside of New Brunswick are required by law to hire guides. These restrictions, along with Fly-fishing Only rules, have helped maintain the quality of the sport, but have contributed much to Atlantic salmon fishing's aura of exclusivity. It almost seemed as if anglers who wanted to fish for Atlantic salmon had to arrange in advance to be born white Anglo-Saxon Protestants, come from old money, graduate from Ivy League colleges, and have jobs as bond traders on Wall Street. On Quebec's Gaspé Peninsula, and on the rivers along the northern shore of the St. Lawrence, many prime beats are available only through lottery drawings, and often reservations are needed one year in advance. While most Quebec rivers are open to the public, most are available only by daily permit, for a fee. More than a hundred Gaspé salmon camps are controlled by clubs and private outfitters. In neighboring Nova Scotia, where most rivers were long ago ruined as salmon fisheries, with only the Margaree and a handful of smaller streams on Cape Breton surviving, all salmon rivers are open to the public, and the visiting angler doesn't need to hire a guide, which means one has to contend with crowds. In Labrador, wilderness fishing trips are an outdoorsman's dream, especially for those able to pay for air service, field camps, outfitters, and guides.

Salmon fishing in Europe can be even more prohibitive. Ireland wrecked its once-legendary salmon and trout rivers with hydro projects, so that today the Emerald Isle is barely fit for fly-fishing. Think of the poems of William Butler Yeats and the fly-fishing scenes in John Ford's *The Quiet Man*, and you'll have an idea what was lost. Irish salmon are in pitiful decline, and commercial salmon farming in the estuaries of Ireland has all but destroyed the once-famous sea-trout fishing there. Scotland's legendary salmon fishing is in dramatic decline, too, with commercial salmon farming taking its toll, although renting a beat on a Scottish salmon river is more expensive than it ever was. Iceland has extraordinary salmon fishing in a treeless, volcanic landscape, but the river beats are in private hands and the cost of even a week's fishing can be very dear. Fishing in Norway is even more expensive, but then you are fishing for the world's largest Atlantic salmon in rivers that pour into Norway's beautiful blue fjords. The only problem is that most of Norway's famous rivers have been almost wiped out by a parasite called *Gyrodactylus salaris*, and many rivers, such as the famous Laerdal, the so-called queen of Norway's salmon rivers, have been purposefully rotenoned in a desperate attempt to wipe out this plague, believed to have come from a hatchery transfer of Baltic Sea salmon. Also, on a number of once-productive wild salmon rivers in Norway, 50 to 80 percent of the fish on the redds in autumn are escapees from the net pens choking the southern coast—an ominous sign for the future of wild salmon.

The world's most prolific runs of Atlantic salmon are found not very far from the reindeer country of Lapland, in rivers on Russia's Kola Peninsula. This is a newly discovered sport fishery. Russian salmon might not be giants, like the fish in Norway, but anglers can wade into rivers such as the Ponoi and

Varzuga and literally yard them out. The Kola rivers spring out of tundra swamps and flow through virgin timberlands, and so far they remain pristine, harassed only by bands of poachers. The Kola Peninsula had been off-limits throughout the Cold War because of the military and radar facilities in Murmansk. When the Iron Curtain came down, the sporting world discovered a previously unguessed-at salmon paradise.

In winter a well-heeled angler can travel to the Southern Hemisphere and experience some of the last unspoiled fishing in interesting places such as Patagonia and Tierra del Fuego. The Chilean coastline is a new fishing frontier, with coastal rivers teeming with salmon and steelhead transplants. Tierra del Fuego has the world's best sea-trout fishing in rivers that flow past windswept ranches called *estancias*. The searun brown trout were transplanted from Europe seven decades ago, and these fish managed to grow to enormous size while living double lives in both fresh and salt water. In slightly less than a human lifetime, this race of searun brown trout had transformed this region into one of the world's greatest anadromous sport fisheries. Now that the wild sea trout are all but gone from the British Isles, the very best of that fishing could today be found under the Southern Cross.

There you have it, a brief overview of the world's remaining salmon and steelhead fishing. In 1086, William the Conqueror ordered a survey of England, listing all landowners and showing the value and extent of their holdings, an inventory that was published as the Domesday Book. I have often imagined a similar, modern inventory for the world's existing salmon and steelhead rivers. The title of that book would indeed have an appropriate double meaning.

Exotic fishing destinations in Europe, Russia, and South America were outside my budget. This was the paradox of my life. I had given up full-time employment in journalism so I would have the leisure time to do the things I like, such as go fishing. But I could barely afford the kind of fishing I most liked. I would have to await a period of greater financial solvency before I would be able to sample Atlantic salmon and sea-trout fishing. But at least I could take advantage of living on the West Coast of America.

I suppose the first place that any serious traveling fly-fisherman dreams about on the West Coast is Alaska. If you want to find rivers that are still in a state of primal wilderness, then Alaska is the place to go. Alaskan rivers are famous for their salmon and rainbow trout. But I was interested in steelhead. The steelhead rivers in the Alaskan panhandle are rather short, and being glacial, they are often turbid and discolored. Alaskan steelhead runs occur in spring and again in autumn. At that northerly latitude, the weather can be dicey. Steelhead swim along the outer coast of Alaska up to Kodiak Island. They do not extend north of that range, as the salmon do. The best Alaskan steelhead fishing is said to take place in silty, serpentine streams in the Aleutian Islands. The Aleutians jut westward into the Bering Sea off the extreme tip of the Alaskan Peninsula. These low islands are as bleak and desolate as landscape ever gets—a true outback. The steelhead fishing can be so good in these short, floodplain rivers, that when the runs are in, fly-fishermen can catch steelhead in numbers undreamed-of else-where. But like most of Alaska, this is strictly fly-in, lodge, and tent-camp fishing.

The Aleutian fish are said to be among the last untainted wild steelhead left in an untouched habitat. Across the cold waters of the Bering Sea lies another of the earth's last truly pristine steelhead habitats. This is the rugged and relatively un-inhabited Kamchatka Peninsula, an eight-hundred-mile-long landmass isolated in the remoteness of Russia's far east, a ter-rain as biologically rich today as it was a thousand years ago. Kamchatka is a breeding ground for waterfowl and shorebirds and half the world's population of Steller's sea eagles. Kam-chatka has more brown bears than Alaska and Canada. A third of all the world's salmonids come out of the peninsula. It is home to the world's greatest concentration of Pacific salmon, as well as steelhead, trout, and char. It is, in fact, the largest single remaining stronghold of wild native salmonid stocks on earth. The rivers on the western shore of the peninsula sustain runs of steelhead, chinook, coho, sockeye, chum, pink, and Asian Masu salmon, as well as resident rainbow trout, Dolly Varden trout, and Asian white-spotted char. It is anybody's guess what riches lie on the eastern shore, as anglers haven't yet explored that side of the peninsula.

Like so many of the world's remaining wild places, Kam-chatka is at a crossroads. This land of volcanoes, lava fields, virgin forests, and braided floodplains is ripe for plunder. Post-Soviet Russia is like Chicago in the Roaring Twenties, subject to a kind of capitalism without the rule of law. It is anybody's guess how long it will take the poachers and environmental despoilers to get their hands on the goodies that Kamchatka has to offer.

A quick look at my bank account determined that I wouldn't be going to Alaska or Kamchatka anytime soon, unless it was with the aid of a Guggenheim grant, and I was fairly certain they didn't give those away for steelhead fishing. Glamour trips weren't within a struggling writer's budget. Those adventures would have to wait for another time. The world of guided trips, heli-fishing, expensive lodges, and fly-in wilderness camps was beyond my means.

The trips I took would have to follow the steelhead bum's practice of driving from river to river in a car that I prayed wouldn't break down, sleeping at moderately priced motels or camping in the woods, eating inexpensive and often bad food, and fishing the rivers mostly on my own.

As fortune would have it, there was just such a trip I could take. And my trip would bring me to the very best steelhead rivers in North America. That place was British Columbia.

There is the belief that those in the past had the best of it. There is the fear that those in the future will have none of it. That's why so many American and European anglers are racing off to fish Alaska and British Columbia, why so many are looking to the Siberian wastelands as their last best hope.

STEELHEAD PARADISE

IN THE SUMMER of 1999, I wrote a letter to Tom Pero informing him that I was going to British Columbia to write a book about wild steelhead in the Pacific Northwest. That I had no particular qualifications to write such a book seemed irrelevant. I wanted to know if Tom had any suggestions for me about places to go, rivers to fish, and people to speak with while I was there. Tom wrote me back, suggesting that I go as his representative for *Wild Steelhead & Salmon*. The magazine (which has since changed its name to *Fly & Fish*) would open doors and provide me opportunities to fish with some of the best-known and most knowledgeable anglers in the steelhead world. And so in mid-September I found myself on the road, bound for British Columbia and the finest steelhead fishing in North America.

I decided to make my trip in autumn, which in British Columbia is prime time for steelhead fishing. In the springtime, along the coast, B.C.'s rivers host tremendous runs of wild steelhead. These rivers get little fanfare and less fishing pressure, at least from visiting anglers. The archipelagoes of British Columbia are teeming with steelhead in short rivers in the

Queen Charlotte Islands, Princess Royal Island, and Vancouver Island. In April steelhead fishermen charter helicopters to fly over the largest temperate rain forest on earth and set them down on remote coastal mountain streams that are impossible to reach on foot.

Newly arrived spring steelhead are among the strongest and brightest steelhead around. There are rivers on Vancouver Island, such as the Stamp, the Ash, and the Cowichan, that offer spring steelhead fishing for the traveling angler. But Vancouver Island, which is well built-up and developed, has been damaged, perhaps irreparably, by extensive clear-cutting of its forests.

On the mainland, in southwestern British Columbia, the Squamish River offers some very fine spring steelhead fishing in April. Farther inland, on tributaries of the mighty Fraser River, streams such as the Vedder, Alouette, and Capilano Rivers enjoy prolific spring runs of steelhead.

But I was interested in the famous steelhead of the Skeena region. There I would find the largest runs in North America on half a dozen of the world's most famous steelhead rivers. Their names—Kispiox, Bulkley, Morice, Babine, Sustut, and Copper—were on the lips of steelhead anglers around the world. It was mid-September, and the Skeena River's run of summer steelhead would have reached these famous tributaries by now. These rivers were their final destinations in a journey that took them from the Pacific Ocean to their spawning beds. I knew that this prime fishing for Skeena steelhead would continue well on into the end of autumn and the onset of British Columbia's early winter. I was arriving at the best time, mid-

September, when things were really getting started, and the weather was still good. A steelhead angler could really lose himself in the Skeena region, spending the better part of autumn driving back and forth among those streams, enjoying some of the best fly-fishing on earth.

British Columbia's size is mind-numbing. From its massive offshore archipelagoes to its Rocky Mountain escarpments, B.C., if set down in the United States, would take up fully one-tenth of our country, yet it has only two percent of our population. The vacant interior plateau is largely mountainous. The escarpments of the Rocky Mountains separate B.C. from the Canadian prairies. The Coastal Range is so rugged and inaccessible that not even a single highway wends its way up British Columbia's spectacular coastline. Because of the mountains, many of the tiny coastal towns can be reached only by boat or seaplane. And many towns within the interior are so small, it is said that when the bus pulls through, the population doubles.

B.C. is the third most populous province in Canada, but that urban sprawl is confined mostly around Vancouver, close by the U.S. border north of Seattle. The rest of the population is spread out rather thinly and also fairly close to the United States border. Because I wanted to get a really good, close-up view of the Canadian Pacific Northwest, I drove rather than flew to my destination, the town of Smithers, in the remoteness of northwestern British Columbia, on the banks of the Bulkley River.

It took me three full days of driving to get to Smithers from my home in San Francisco. When I crossed over the Canadian border at Lynden, Washington, I actually had to turn eastward into the province rather than drive northwest toward my destination. The Coast Mountains blocked the way. Because the interior plateau is so mountainous, the rivers provide the only low-level passages through it. And so I drove east for a long time along the broad, alluvial plain of the Fraser Valley, before finally turning north up into the steep canyons of the Fraser and Thompson Rivers.

I followed the highway along the canyon of the Fraser, British Columbia's longest river. Salmon swim 850 miles up the Fraser, one of the longest spawning migrations in North America. A pity that the once-great salmon and steelhead runs on the Fraser have been sacrificed to dams. With the fish runs on the Fraser and our own mighty Columbia diminished by hydropower projects, the Skeena was now the world's major steelhead artery. I looked down at the sunlit Fraser, broad and powerful, colored by a turbid suspension of glacial-rock flour that left the green-tinted water slightly clay-colored. Both the Fraser and the Mackenzie, Canada's longest river, have their headwaters in northern British Columbia, with the glacial snow of Mount Robson, highest peak in the Canadian Rockies, serving as the headwater source of the Fraser.

In time the alpine scenery I was enjoying began to give way to high desert. A steep canyon of hair-raising curves took me up into the tributary of the Thompson River. Looking down into the gorge, I saw a river as powerful as the Fraser, maybe more so. The river looked rather fearsome, its white foaming rapids seemingly impassable in places. The world's strongest steelhead swam up the Thompson to spawn. They had to be strong in order to mount the ferocious rapids as well as get by the narrow, steep-sided canyon farther downriver known as Hells Gate, through which the combined waters of the Thompson and Fraser Rivers roared.

I was looking at a brown and largely treeless landscape, bare slopes that made the Thompson River appear even more forbidding. Sparse belts of pine brought a little relief to the eye, but all in all this was sagebrush country. I was looking at the very northernmost tip of the great North American desert. I had come into a country of rain shadow lying behind the mountains, a dry ranchland of blowing tumbleweeds and desert steppes. The high-desert landscape gave the Thompson River a raw, incomplete look, not at all to my liking.

Big landscape, big river, big steelhead. Come November, fly-fishermen would be converging on the Thompson, on places such as the sweeping expanse of the Graveyard Pool, where they would fish for the river's mighty steelhead. Treadmill testing in laboratories had determined that these were indeed the world's strongest steelhead, able to hold their own against an unrelenting current twice as long as steelhead from other rivers. These Thompson fish had evolved into brutes, adapting to those frightening whitewater rapids that distinguished the Thompson. On average, Thompson steelhead might weigh about fifteen pounds, with many going into the twenties. They are not the world's largest steelhead—those are to be found in the Kispiox and Babine Rivers. But the Thompson fish are incredible battlers. In fact, it is said that the only other steelhead comparable to Thompson River fish in the kind of fight they put up are found in the Dean River, on the central coast of British Columbia. The Dean is accessible only by boat or helicopter, and frankly it would have been my first choice to fish had I been able to swing a trip up there. I had heard many rapturous stories about the legendary fishing on the Dean. And I had seen photographs of the river, too, with its gravel bars shining in the sun, evergreen forests, and huge glacial mountains rising above the river valley. Certainly the Dean River had one of the most impressive backdrops imaginable for steelhead fishing. Grizzly bears wandered its banks, and Dean anglers battled steelhead that were just a few days out of the ocean, which was why they felt so strong on rod and reel. Dean River fish were said to be the best-looking searun fish in British Columbia. Dean River steelhead were not quite as large as Thompson River fish, but felt just as strong. This might be a different story if Thompson anglers weren't fighting steelhead that had swum three hundred river miles from the salt, spending months in the lower Fraser River.

I found the high-desert landscape rather ugly and uninviting. The Thompson River country has endured abuse from heavy logging and cattle ranching. The hills looked badly overgrazed. But the fishing around the town of Spences Bridge was said to be world-class. Perhaps on my return home, I would have a chance to fish the famous Graveyard Pool. The good fishing on the Thompson doesn't really begin until November anyway. Incredibly, Thompson River steelhead rise to dry flies when river temperatures are barely above freezing. Thompson steelhead smolts spend two years in the river before heading out to sea, feeding on insects, snapping at the millions of three-inch stoneflies that live in the river. When they return from the Pacific Ocean—two, three, and even four years later in some cases—they haven't forgotten how to chase insects. The Thompson is a river for serious steelhead anglers only. The basketball-size stones carpeting the river bottom create what might be the most dangerous wading in steelhead fishing.

I spent the night in Cache Creek, a dusty ranching town where Sikhs in turbans operate the convenience stores. I wondered what they thought of cowboys, ranching, and the music of Ian Tyson. As I drove north the next day, the sagebrush disappeared and the alpine scenery quickly returned. It remined me in some ways of Montana. I continued on through the high plains and forests of the interior plateau, until arriving at last at the town of Prince George, at the very center of British Columbia. Prince George seemed to spring out of nowhere. Once strictly a railroad and timber town, it had become the third-largest city in British Columbia, with a population of about seventy thousand people, a modern burg complete with shopping malls and a bustling town center. Prince George was officially known as the "Western White Spruce Capital of the World," a center for wood processing and pulp production. The Nechako River, flowing down from the northwest, joined the Fraser at Prince George. The city was a hub of humanity in the center of a wilderness.

I headed northwest on the Yellowhead Highway, into the heart of the so-called Lakes District of British Columbia. It had been named after England's famous Lakes District, but no one was about to mistake this for one of Britain's pastoral theme parks. Here was an immense forest and ranching country so incomprehensibly huge it swallowed up three hundred lakes.

At the end of a very long day, I arrived at my destination,

the Bulkley Valley. This marked a kind of border between the interior plateau of British Columbia and the giant coastal fir forests of the Pacific Northwest, waiting on the other side of the Bulkley Range. Driving into the town of Houston, the first thing I spotted were roadside banners festooned with symbols of leaping steelhead. Earlier in the century, the tiny settlement of Houston had been established as a tie-cutting center for the Grand Trunk Pacific Railway. These days forestry, ranching, and mining provided the main sources of employment for the town's thirty-six hundred or so residents; and steelhead and coho fishing provided its main sources of pleasure.

A lot of my ideas about this part of British Columbia had come from my reading two books, Edward Hoagland's *Notes from the Century Before*, and John F. Fennelly's *Steelhead Paradise*, both written near the mid–twentieth century. Hoagland is a master of the personal essay. Fennelly's book describes steelhead fishing at a time when the rivers were a secret known only to a handful of intrepid fly-fishermen. Fennelly was an American investment banker who chartered bush planes to get himself and his fishing cronies into this steelhead Eden. He first laid eyes on the Skeena country on a misty morning in September 1951, when his chartered Grumman Goose floatplane dropped him and his companions off on Morice Lake, a sapphire jewel surrounded by a trackless forest. Snowcapped mountains rose on three sides of their camp and the nearest road was fifty miles away. Fennelly found fishing like it must have been at the dawn of man. Except for some Indian villages and a few small towns along the railroad, there was little but wilderness up there.

Fennelly had an interesting career, and despite his rather privileged background, he seemed like a regular guy. He served as a flying cadet during World War One, and at Princeton he had been the school's welterweight boxing champion. He worked briefly as a magazine editor and a newspaper reporter, taught economics for a short time at Columbia University in New York, and entered the investment-banking business in 1929, just in time for the Great Crash. Despite his investment duties, he also found time to direct a string of corporations, including an oil company. During World War Two, he served on the staff of the War Production Board in Washington, D.C., where he was responsible for the allocation and distribution of war materials. He co-authored the book *Fiscal Planning for Total War*, a volume that enjoyed a somewhat shorter shelf life than *Steelhead Paradise*. Although he was an investment banker, he didn't seem particularly interested in accumulating wealth for himself, and he had fairly simple tastes overall. He viewed materialism as a dead end. "A man is wealthy in my book," he wrote in *Steelhead Paradise*, "if he has sufficient resources within himself to enjoy the simple pleasures in life, and live well within the limits of moderate circumstances. Thus, if his tastes and material desires are simple enough, one individual with a small capital may actually be wealthier than another who has several millions, but who feels compelled to spend more and more in lavish living as his fortune increases."

Fennelly came to fly-fishing rather late in life, while he was in his mid-forties, working as a bureaucrat in Washington and pondering what he was going to do in his spare time when the war ended. He turned to the fly rod only after he realized that his golf game wasn't going to get any better as he got older. He never considered himself to be anything other than an amateur fly-fisherman, and he endeared himself to me when he wrote in *Steelhead Paradise* that "[b]ecause it is a factual history, it is a report of at least as many failures as strikes."

It has occurred to me that the author of *Steelhead Paradise* and I share a few things in common. We both came to fly fishing late (me at age twenty-seven), and we both taught ourselves how to use a fly rod (in my case poorly); we had both been newspapermen; we shared a love of poetry; we both lived in cities and rather enjoyed them, but felt a need to escape to the outdoors. The great difference between us (other than his conservatism and my anarchist politics) was the fact that we were separated by a half-century. I was exactly six months old when Fennelly had first set down in British Columbia. And I knew I would never get to see the pristine wilderness exactly as Fennelly had found it. Even Fennelly saw what was coming, and he predicted that the Skeena's youthful blush would fade within a few decades.

Fennelly's search for refreshment in nature took him from trout streams in Montana, and Atlantic salmon rivers in the Maritimes and Iceland, to the steelhead rivers of the Skeena wilderness. As he put it, he was looking for a place to go fishing where there were no automobiles or hard-surfaced roads, and he found it. In all, he made six trips to British Columbia over the period of a decade. His fishing buddies were a varied crew that included a taxi driver in Smithers and the American lawyer John Marshall Harlan, who almost died of a bleeding ulcer one night in camp, but lived to be appointed a justice of the United

States Supreme Court. Fennelly was acutely aware that in British Columbia he had found one of the world's last fly-fishing frontiers. He couldn't believe the numbers of steelhead he caught. In a single two-week period while fishing the Sustut and Johanson Rivers, Fennelly's party landed a hundred steelhead among them and, except for a few they ate, returned the majority to the water. Fennelly himself managed to land nineteen fish, including a seventeen-pounder. Fennelly wrote *Steelhead Paradise* simply to please himself and to record the splendor of his environs and the sport he found there. Steelhead fishermen are much in his debt.

The only other books I had read about the fishing in British Columbia were those written by Roderick Haig-Brown. No other fishing writer in our time has had a better critical reception than Roderick Langmere Haig-Brown, the patron saint of modern fly-fishing writers. At age twenty Haig-Brown, an Englishman, emigrated to Vancouver Island to work as a roughneck and a logger in the great forests of the Pacific Northwest. He went on to become a practicing magistrate, a chancellor of the University of Victoria, a conservationist of much stature, and a writer of many books. He was that ideal combination of a man of action and of letters. He left behind a large body of work that showed his wide-ranging interests—twenty-eight published books in all, both fiction and nonfiction—but he is best known as a fishing writer. Haig-Brown's fishing books are viewed as high literature, as least by fly-fishermen. But I'd never gotten a strong visual sense out of his prose; and I had little clear idea from reading his books what his mountains and rivers might look like. Haig-Brown made his home in the tiny town of Campbell River on Vancouver Island, and he fished and wrote mostly about his home streams. If he ever visited the Skeena region to fish, he never wrote about it. So the Fennelly book was really going to have to serve as my Baedeker on this trip.

I knew better—knew I wasn't going to find those rugged outposts described in the Fennelly and Hoagland books. And yet I still wasn't prepared for the degree to which the Bulkley Valley appeared to be built-up and tamed. I think I was expecting a little more of the sense of isolation, and maybe a little something of the frontier hardship experienced at midcentury. But the Bulkley Valley looked downright comfortable to live in.

The Bulkley River was accessible by paved roads for most of its length. (Only a hard-to-reach stretch of canyon could be considered true wilderness.) The Bulkley River flows past the towns of Telkwa and Smithers toward a confluence with the Skeena under three snowcapped ranges, the Bulkleys, the Babines, and the Hazeltons. The river has a reputation as relatively easy to wade or float by driftboat (except in the canyon, where it can get kind of hairy). Because of its accessibility, and because fully half of the Skeena's steelhead spawn in the Bulkley, or go upstream to spawn in the Morice River, the Bulkley is an ideal river for anglers who couldn't afford wilderness lodges or fly-out trips, but rather planned to camp or take advantage of moderately priced motel lodging. There is no shortage of motor-home and tent camping in the area. The Bulkley, like the nearby Kispiox, was made for steelhead bums, those individuals so possessed that they do little else in life but fish, having forsaken jobs and families to pitch tents and live off canned beans in their pursuit of anadromous wonder fish. These fishing hermits make up a certain hard-core fraternity among fly-fishermen, and their like can be found from the steelhead rivers of British Columbia to the Rocky Mountain trout streams of Montana and Wyoming. In pursuing a sport to the mindless exclusion of nearly everything else, they manage to achieve something that so far has eluded the majority of us—a life of radical freedom. But like Kurtz in *Heart of Darkness*, some of them have gone too far up the river.

When I reached the town of Telkwa, a whistle-stop settlement between Houston and Smithers, I turned into the Douglas Motel, a fishing resort overlooking a stretch of the Bulkley River broken by a small rapid and a gravel-bar island. My room had been booked for me in advance by my host, the Northern British Columbia Tourism Association. I stepped into the office to check in, and the first thing I got was an earful from Maxine Douglas, who runs the motel with her husband, Hugh.

"The last writer for *Wild Steelhead & Salmon* came up here and he claimed that there were no fish in the Bulkley!" Maxine exclaimed, momentarily forgetting that Canadians are required by law to be overly polite. This is the first thing Americans notice about being in Canada: everyone is so well behaved. The national temperament seems as bland as the cooking. British Columbians are especially nice to strangers. Maybe it has something to do with the immensity of their province and the fact that there really aren't enough of them to get on each other's nerves. In a vast mountainous province that is two-thirds trees, where folks can be cut off for days from the rest of the world by a landslide or a snowfall, hospitality and kindness toward your fellow man can come in handy. Canadians are at the mercy of their continent and their weather more than Americans are. Whatever the reason—whether the remoteness or the inhospitable climate—Canadians are famously tolerant, painfully considerate, and unreasonably even-tempered. Americans are prone to think of Canadians, if we think of them at all, only in clichés. My favorite is the definition of a Canadian as someone who can have sex in a canoe.

Apparently Maxine's placid Canadian temperament had been stretched to the breaking point. It was plain to me that she had been waiting all day for an opportunity to speak her mind. Perhaps she had been waiting all year.

"That writer said the Thompson River was the most beautiful whore he had ever met!" Maxine exclaimed. "We put up those two guys and paid for all their meals and *this* is what they wrote?"

Whoa. *Whores* on the Thompson River? What was this lady talking about? Now, there was one magazine story that I would have to read. Actually, I did read the story some time later on. Apparently Maxine had confused her freeloading journalist with an entirely different correspondent for the magazine, Ehor Boyanowsky, a professor who teaches criminal psychology at Simon Fraser University in Vancouver in the spare moments when he isn't fly-fishing. Boyanowsky had written a story that was part memoir, recounting how after the breakup of his first marriage many years ago, he had sought sweet anodyne in a trip to the Bulkley River. Finding no fish in the Bulkley that year due to rapacious gill-netting by a commercial salmon fleet at the mouth of the Skeena River, Boyanowsky fled south to the Thompson, where he discovered the kind of steelhead fishing that changes a man's life. In the article that so upset Maxine, Boyanowsky quoted a remark made to him by a veteran Skeena steelhead fisherman, one Jimmy Wright, a former San Francisco bank executive, who gave up banking to go steelhead fishing, lucky man, and who surprised the writer by telling him that the Thompson was his favorite river. " 'It's like a beautiful whore,' " Boyanowsky quoted Jimmy Wright as saying. " 'Once she's got you, regardless of how badly she treats you, how she seems to prefer undeserving louts, you're hooked.' " Maxine had totally misread the article. After I related this incident to him, Tom Pero told me: "Now you know the kind of shit I have to put up with."

I was following in the wake of fishing journalists whose articles weren't always going to please the business community. And who could blame the outfitters and lodge owners? Writing for fishing publications might be the last source of legitimate graft left in journalism. Autumn is a critical time for steelhead camp operators and lodge owners in this part of British Columbia, and these people have only a short time to earn a living and make a success of their businesses. They really couldn't afford the luxury of hosting some parasitic writer and taking him out for free on an expensive guided trip when they were scrambling to accommodate actual paying customers. But they did it anyway, often cheerfully, and it was inevitable that a few wouldn't always be pleased with what got reported.

Tom Pero had written me a letter of introduction, which in its diplomatic subtlety would have been worthy of someone working for the U.S. State Department. He had asked the

Northern British Columbia Tourism Association for any help the agency could provide in arranging for my lodging and meals, and maybe a few river trips with the guides. In his letter Tom stressed that I wasn't out here expecting to take up space in an expensive lodge or compete with paying clients for standard "rotation" beats on float trips. But Tom suggested that I might be allowed to tag along on the occasional river float if there was an empty seat available in the driftboat. I could watch and mostly take notes, and listen to the guides and the camp owners tell me the story of British Columbia steelhead fishing from their unique perspective. It was a tricky business. During my stay I found that many of the outfitters who offered to take me out and show me their rivers would have to cancel abruptly because of last-minute bookings from paying guests. And this was only right. The last thing any lodge owner or outfitter needed was a day spent in the great outdoors entertaining a freebooting writer. And yet I was quite touched by the number of people who offered to host me.

In fact, Marilyn Quilley, the general manager of the Northern British Columbia Tourism Association, had already lined up a number of folks eager to host me on their streams. Collin Schadrech, at Farwest Steelhead Lodge here in Telkwa, wanted to take me on a float down the Bulkley. Ray's Fly Fishing in Houston had offered to introduce me to steelhead fishing on the Morice River. Noel Gyger, who operates Northwest Fishing Guides in Terrace, wanted to take me on a float trip on the Skeena. The people at Northland Steelhead Lodge on the Bulkley River, just outside the town of Smithers, would try to fit me into their schedule; and the folks at Skeena Wilderness Fishing in Terrace were talking about taking me on a two-day trip somewhere nice. There was even some talk about a possible helicopter ride to a remote coastal stream. And best of all, the hosts of Babine Steelhead Lodge had offered to put me up in their wilderness lodge on the river for a few nights. Little did I know at the time that most of these people would cancel so I would pretty much be fishing on my lonesome in the ensuing days.

Sooner or later everyone who is anyone in the steelhead fishing world winds up on the Bulkley River. "Oh, you just missed Jack Hemingway," Maxine told me. Maxine was a delightful host now that she had gotten what she wanted to say off her chest. "Jack just left for the Kispiox River," she told me, disappointed that the two of us weren't able to meet. I was disappointed, too, as Jack Hemingway was a legend among steelhead fishermen. As I was checking in to my riverfront cabin, the fellow in the cabin next to mine, Bill Levine, from Livingston, Montana, told me that Russell Chatham was to have come up with him but had had to cancel at the last minute to attend to a personal matter.

That night I had steelhead fever. For a long while I lay awake in bed, anticipating the dawn. I had set aside the next morning for exploring the Bulkley River on my own and getting my first taste of its famous steelhead fishing. But first a short drive north up the highway to the town of Smithers seemed in order.

Smithers is a small burg of about 5,600 souls nestled at the base of Hudson Bay Mountain. Located exactly halfway between Prince Rupert on the coast and Prince George in the interior, Smithers had gotten its start as the divisional headquarters of the Grand Trunk Pacific Railway, and the town was even named after the railroad's chairman, A. W. Smithers. In time a logging community grew up around the railroad depot. These days Smithers is more a playground for fly-fishermen, rockhounds, whitewater rafters, skiers, and other outdoors types. The town has a vaguely Bavarian look that comes from the faux chalet architecture. Although the town is old, most of its business district looks as if it was built during the last fifteen minutes. Hudson Bay Mountain looms over the town, its four separate peaks dominating all views from the lower valley. If I lived here, I would probably spend half my working hours gazing at Hudson Bay's incredible hanging glacier.

Smithers immediately put me in mind of West Yellowstone, Montana, the town that sprang to life around the western entrance to Yellowstone National Park. Not that the two towns look in any way alike. But both are famous fishing outposts. Within a hundred-mile radius of West Yellowstone are the best trout streams in the United States outside of Alaska. And within a half-day's drive of Smithers are seven of the nine best steelhead rivers in Canada. (The Thompson and the Dean lie outside the Skeena system.)

But unlike West Yellowstone, which has five full-time fly shops, Smithers has none. And so I paid a visit to a general sporting-goods store in the commercial district, to buy a handful of suitable steelhead flies for the Bulkley. Earlier I had purchased my license and fishing permits from Hugh and Maxine back at the motel. Most fishing lodges sell licenses as well as the required daily permits fishermen must obtain in order to get on the classified waters. It costs a non-Canadian angler $55 for an annual fishing license. There is also a separate $40 fee for a steelhead permit. And then there are those special permits for the classified rivers. A Class One river would set an angler back $20 a day; a Class Two river, $10. This is not a commentary on how good the fishing can be on these rivers; rather, it defines the experience. The fishing on the Bulkley River, a Class Two stream, might be every bit as good as the fishing on the Babine, a Class One river. But the Class One designation is reserved for those wilderness streams like the Babine that are not accessible by any paved road. Presumably one is paying extra for the wilderness experience.

In recent years, foreign anglers had been allowed to fish all the B.C. rivers anytime, anyplace, simply for the price of an annual fishing license. But of late the pressure had grown so great in the province that now anglers were required to pay daily fees in order to get on the choicest streams. Still it was the cheapest such fishing for salmonids available in Canada. The fees to fish Atlantic salmon rivers in the eastern Maritimes were far more expensive, and on some of those Atlantic salmon beats, anglers were required by law to hire guides for a day astream. There was nothing like that going on in British Columbia, yet. But that day probably wasn't far off. As pressure to fish in British Columbia mounts, there can be little doubt that B.C. will be forced to adopt the kind of expensive and exclusionary restrictions that long have been the custom on Canada's lordly Atlantic salmon rivers.

I had to ask around in order to find access routes down to the river. The Bulkley, or what I saw of it from Telkwa downstream to Smithers, seemed a little too built-up and developed to suit my tastes. The houses along the banks seemed inappropriate. This wasn't my idea of wilderness fishing at all. But then, this was no longer the river as John Fennelly saw it.

I followed the directions Maxine and Hugh had given me, and halfway between Smithers and Telkwa, I found a turnoff marked Donaldson Road and drove down it. I came to another street where I could park in a vacant field opposite some houses. From there I followed a footpath through the trees until I came out on a long gravel bar beside the river. I rigged up with a great feeling of excitement and anticipation.

The river was the color of a blended margarita. I would later learn that the green stain was the result of a rain that had fallen on the Telkwa glacier, far upstream. The Telkwa River, which empties into the Bulkley just above the Douglas Motel, was the villain in this drama. Its green-tinted outpour flowed into the Bulkley, discoloring everything downstream. Had I known enough to fish the Bulkley above the town of Telkwa, I would have found clearer water. But this green bar drink looked okay to me. After all, I was a California steelhead fisherman, and every winter I fished in rivers that were the color of avocados. I thought this color was natural. But another angler I met walking along the gravel bar set me straight. "The fishing's off," he warned. "The river's too green."

Still, it seemed clear enough to me. I could make out my boots down there on the streambed, barely. I knew it was fly-fishable. That's the rule: If you can see your boots on the bottom, you can fly-fish. I waded out into the streaming water, and began to work my way down a long run, casting and watching my riffle-hitched fly skittering across the surface. The current felt good around my legs. Here I was, fishing in Canada at last.

By hiking upstream along the gravel bar, I had managed to get away from the views of most of the houses. It was as if they had somehow receded back into the original wilderness. The cottonwoods and alders along the bank burned an autumn saffron and looked unusually brilliant against the blue-green water. A sharp scent of pine came out of the forest.

Well downstream, I watched another angler mending line with what appeared to be a sixteen-foot medieval lance. It was a Spey rod—one of those two-handed salmon sticks that made a big comeback among fly-fishermen in recent years. Back in the nineteenth century, they were the rod of choice for salmon fishermen in the British Isles. They never really went out of favor over there in Europe. But in the United States, shorter rods were seen as easier to handle, and somehow more like real fly-fishing. John Fennelly made fun of them—he called them "telegraph poles." In his day, American salmon and steelhead fishermen used single-handed rods exclusively, and when they traveled abroad they were laughed at for their short rods by European anglers. Only within the last decade had West Coast steelhead fishermen begun adopting the Spey rod as the rod of choice for their big rivers. Every year there seemed to be more Spey rods on the water. Now they were all the rage among West Coast steelhead fishermen, and many North American Atlantic salmon fishermen were taking them up, too. It wasn't really a question of casting farther. A really good caster (and I certainly didn't qualify in that department) could cast almost as far with a single-hander as with a Spey rod. But Spey casting, which involves a kind of elaborate roll cast and requires no backcast at all, allows fly-fishermen to fish runs they never could fish before because of obstructions along the bank. Using a Spey rod virtually doubles the amount of water an angler can fish. Another advantage of the Spey rod is that with the extra reach, one can better mend line and control the fly's drift than with a single-handed rod.

I hadn't yet tried fishing with a Spey rod. That cast is made in a kind of figure-8 motion and, as I understand it, uses the tension from the line on the water to load the rod. All the people I saw doing it made it look easy. But it would require my learning a whole new way of casting and thinking, and I felt I wasn't ready for that yet. Besides, I prefer to confine my mediocrity to a single discipline rather than spread it around. But the single best argument I could think of against taking up Spey casting is that I would have to spend money I didn't have, buying myself a brand-new outfit that I couldn't afford.

In order to celebrate my Canadian trip, I had purchased a new Scott rod. If that sounds contradictory, let's just say I've had my eye on that rod for a long time. True, it cost me five times more than what I'd paid for a semester of English Lit back when I was in college. But I saw the Scott as the ideal steelhead rod. It was nine-and-a-half feet long and designed to throw an 8-weight line. Light enough, yet with something down its pants, so to speak. Over the years I had cast various generations of this rod as they were owned by my friends. It tracked beautifully and was smoother than almost any other 8-weight rod I had ever cast. But I really hadn't been able to afford it—a new rod wasn't within my budget. Finally I threw fiscal responsibility aside and bought the rod to celebrate my trip to British Columbia. I couldn't afford the trip, either, so I figured what the hell—in for a dime, in for a dollar. I was looking forward to christening my new rod with my first Canadian steelhead.

A hundred casts later, nothing had happened. In steelhead fishing, each cast is placed a few feet farther downstream than the last. You cast across stream, or slightly down, and then let your line swing downstream until it completes a quarter-circle. Then, when it is hanging directly below you, the fly fluttering at the end of it, you pick it up, step down, and repeat the maneuver all over again. In this kind of fishing, your mind can do as much drifting as your line. That's why steelhead fishing requires just as much concentration as it does patience (to say nothing of a capacity for dull, repetitive motion). Your senses are lulled by the sounds of the river and the pull of the current and soon your mind is wandering downstream like a leaf on the water. But the Bulkley was no river for woolgathering. When a steelhead hits, one has to be ready. Even more than concentration, steelhead fishing requires a kind of stubborn perseverance. You have to get used to the idea that you might never catch a fish. You have to steel yourself to the possibility that you might spend two whole weeks in some place as glorious as British Columbia and never catch a single steelhead. Believe me, even the excitement of being on a new river will wane if there isn't any action.

But suddenly I see something happening upstream from me. It appears that another angler has a steelhead jumping on the end of his line. This is indeed a good sign. The fish is thrashing around wildly. From where I stand, I can hear the reel whirring. When the steelhead jumps and the line falls slack, I think the fish has come off. But no, it has only changed direction, and now the angler is reeling like mad to pick up the slack. Finally, with much of the long belly of line back in the reel, the rod begins quivering and dancing once again. The steelhead leads the angler downstream, so that he is coming closer to me, giving me a good view of the action. I see him stumble once over a sunken rock, but he recovers his balance. The fish is really pulling him around, leading him over the rocks. I reel in my line, in case I have to give way to him and his fish. This is really quite thrilling.

Finally the fish is wallowing in the shallows. But the moment the steelhead feels the gravel on its belly, it lunges away in one last attempt to get to open water. For a moment I think the angler is going to lose him. But no, the fellow keeps pressure on the rod, and soon the steelhead is beached. (I should point out that in steelhead fishing, "beaching" doesn't mean dragging a steelhead out of the water where it is allowed to flop all over the rocks, possibly hurting itself. It simply means bringing a subdued fish into the shallows where it can be easily handled in quiet water.) I watch the fisherman lean over to loosen his fly from the steelhead's jaw. In a moment he is setting free ten pounds of streaming henfish.

I congratulated the angler and in our ensuing conversation I asked him where he was from. When he told me he was from the San Francisco Bay Area, I wasn't surprised. The novelist Thomas McGuane has observed that the reason one sees so many San Franciscans scattered so widely throughout steelhead country is because our home fishery is all but extinct. The fellow told me he flew here and was planning to fish for an entire week before returning to his job. He acknowledged that the fishing had been slow; he'd only had four hookups all morning. Was this guy for real? I'd gone an entire year once with only four hookups.

"This is my first time in B.C.," I told him. "I don't even know if I'm doing this right. Let me ask you something: am I wading out far enough?"

"Don't go in over your knees," the fellow said, providing me with the most useful and memorable piece of advice I was to hear during my entire stay in British Columbia. "If you're wading up to your nuts, you're too deep."

He explained that the steelhead were lying fairly close to the bank. In the low light of early morning and evening, they'd move in even closer. As the sun climbed higher, they'd move out a little bit farther, but not very far. Things were different up here, he explained. This wasn't California. It was no longer necessary to wade out chest-high and cast a hundred feet of line. He said that if I waded out too deeply here, I'd be stepping on the steelhead.

The Bulkley had a reputation as an easy river to wade, and I was finding it so. Keeping close by the bank would make it even easier. Tom Pero had cautioned me that I might want to get a wading staff for some of these big rivers. He warned me that the currents could be strong and treacherous. But I had never used a staff, not even for the tricky wading required on the North Umpqua River back in Oregon. And I wasn't about to start now. Wading staffs cost about $50 or $60, a lot of money for a stick of wood.

I stripped out a lot of line from my reel and made a few false casts. From where I stood I could see one or two houses visible from behind the screen of trees. No, this part of the Bulkley couldn't be considered a wilderness. But it was the next best thing. And all I had to do was look up at the mountains and know that the wilderness was out there all around me, going off in all directions. There wasn't a single dam on the Bulkley. The river rose and fell with nature's moods, not with electric switches. Rainfall and snowmelt determined how the river flowed. And there were no hatcheries—all the steelhead were wild. They had been born out of snowmelt, in a stream rather than in a concrete holding tank. It would be sheer ingratitude to complain about a few houses in sight along the river. I lifted my rod smoothly, raising several feet of line off the sliding current, looping it back upstream with a counterclockwise roll of my wrist, putting a mend in the line to keep it from bellying.

Seeing how much habitation there was along this stretch of the Bulkley between Telkwa and Smithers, I was all the more impressed that the river had never been dammed. Back in the 1950s, the world's largest aluminum company, Alcan, had planned to create a giant reservoir in the headwaters of the Morice and Bulkley Rivers that would divert water for hydropower and smelting. While he was fishing the Morice River, John Fennelly had come across two Alcan employees scouting possible sites for the dam around Morice Lake. When he caught these sons-of-bitches shooting a bald eagle, he read the pair the riot act. The Canadian government had gone so far as to sign water agreements with Alcan for the project. But the citizens of British Columbia rose up in protest. An epic twenty-year environmental battle ensued. Somewhat astonishingly, Alcan, with all its political clout and money, lost. Even British Columbia's conservative Liberal Party (for some reason the right wing in B.C. is called "Liberal") came out against the behemoth project. Canadian conservatives hadn't forgotten they had something valuable to conserve, a lesson that has been lost on conservatives in the United States.

Thankfully, there were no steelhead hatcheries up here, either. In the United States, fisheries managers had their heads stuck in a hatchery philosophy that created political jobs, endless funding, and a self-perpetuating bureaucracy. Hatchery fish were a pathetic simulacrum of nature, hardly a replacement for the loss of habitat. But hatcheries weren't financially feasible this far up in British Columbia because rivers at this northerly latitude were simply too cold. A hatchery smolt is bred to swim out to sea in one year. Because of the colder water temperatures, a steelhead's pre-migrant life in these rivers can be as long as five years.

I fished through the drift attentively, working around a few sunken rocks. Easing my way downstream into the tailout, I was careful to fish each swing of the fly all the way out until it held directly below me. Then I'd wait a few seconds as the fly hung teasingly in the current, and I'd strip in a few feet, always hoping that a steelhead was just waiting to pounce on the fly. Sometimes steelhead will follow a fly until it stops, dangling in the current, and then attack it the moment it begins to move again, when the angler begins to strip in line.

As I waded, I searched out firm footholds among the cobblestones. The current was easy; the wading comfortable. The river's low gradient and shallow channels made wading relatively easy. Most of the time I was fishing a dry fly on the surface of the river, my favorite method because it is so visual. The fly was large and bushy and no doubt it cast a good silhouette on top of the water. A fish looking up from relative darkness into relative brightness would have no trouble seeing it. Any moment now, I expected the fly to disappear in a swirl, a big watery boil caused by a rising steelhead. I used my rod tip to tease the fly, skittering it back and forth across the smooth current. I wanted to feel the tug of life on my line, feel a steelhead transmit its energy up to me through the rod.

I threw long casts across the river, backed by alders and cottonwoods that were like candle flames reflecting in the blue-green water. If I have learned any one thing from fishing, it is that I like autumn best. Roderick Haig-Brown observed that, more than any other time of the year, autumn is the season of movement. Every living thing in the sky and in the water is on the move.

As the sun tracked lower in the sky, the air grew chillier. The river felt particularly bracing now. I accelerated my line speed with a smooth, fast stroke called a double-haul and delivered my cast as far as I could get it. Although I was wading near shore, I wanted these casts to cover as much water as possible. I wasn't yet convinced that all the fish would be close to the bank. I mended my line at the moment the cast settled onto the water, and then gave it a second upstream flip just to be sure. The purpose of mending is to prevent line from bellying in the current, causing the fly to come around too fast. In mid-drift I'd start mending line again, either to correct the swing, or to pop the fly and give it a little action.

The afternoon was ending too quickly for me. A blue haze was visible on the air and its vapor quickly chilled me. There was an evanescence of mist all around. A cold dusk was settling into the valley. The dimming light drained the bulk from the mountains. Oddly, the chill did little to draw the moisture out of the air.

It was dark now, and through the trees I saw headlights jerking up and down as departing pickups drove away over the uneven ground. My fellow fishermen were calling it quits for the evening.

I'd like to say that in those final moments of dusk, when all my expectations were riding at their highest, I hooked and landed my first British Columbia steelhead, on this, my first day of fishing in Canada. I'd even be content to say that I felt the tug of a steelhead momentarily on my line before it spit out the hook. But I cannot tell a lie. To borrow a line from Nick Carraway, my hero in *The Great Gatsby*, everyone suspects himself of at least one of the cardinal virtues, and this is mine: I am one of the few honest fishermen I have ever known.

BEARS WITH MY FISHING

I T WAS DIFFICULT to sleep that night, with my head filled with thoughts of a float trip on the Bulkley River. And so I was up in the predawn blackness, getting myself ready. At first light, I found myself driving down the dim streets of Telkwa, looking for the old creamery building that had been converted into Farwest Steelhead Lodge.

Five minutes later I was sitting down to an elaborate breakfast inside the lodge. This was the kind of place that tended to attract serious fishermen. The dining room bustled with the clatter of plates and silverware as fishermen and fisherwomen sat down to platters of sausages, pancakes, oatmeal, and fresh fruit, stoking themselves for a big day on the river. Everyone was unusually cheerful and enthusiastic. I'd never seen so many people so happy to be up so early in the morning.

"So what do you plan to write about?" Collin Schadrech, the owner of the lodge, asked me. I got the feeling that he was sizing me up. Collin had invited me for a day on the river as his personal guest. This had been arranged through the good graces of Marilyn Quilley at the Northern British Columbia Tourism Association. Collin had a neatly trimmed salt-and-pepper beard and he appeared to me to be exceptionally trim and fit for a middle-aged man. That probably had something to do with rowing driftboats on big Canadian rivers. He and his wife Shari lived in the main lodge, which was also their home. They had been operating their lodge here on the south bank of the Bulkley River since 1981, having completely refurbished the creamery that once stood here.

"Well, this is my first time in British Columbia," I told Collin, launching into my carefully prepared speech. "These rivers are completely new to me. I want to get a firsthand understanding of the Bulkley and learn about the steelhead fishing up here. But most of all I want to know what kind of future the steelhead have in British Columbia."

"Then let's get you on the river," Collin said.

From the lodge, through the screen of cottonwoods bordering the banks, I had seen the greenish Telkwa River emptying into the larger and clearer Bulkley. The two rivers flowed side by side for a short ways, quite distinguishable from one another. Collin informed our group that the Bulkley below the Telkwa was discolored from the rain that had fallen on a glacial mountain above the Telkwa River several days earlier. Because the green tint was affecting visibility on the Bulkley below the confluence, we would fish above it. Our destination was Walcott, about twenty miles upstream of the lodge. We would launch our driftboats there.

We put on our waders and assembled our rods, stashing them in the vehicle that would transport us to the river. The morning was overcast and foggy and I was still half asleep. The light, which seemed to be coming not so much out of the east as from some directionless nowhere, wasn't growing brighter, only increasing by amount. Collin said the low overcast would probably burn off by the time we got under way on the river.

His words proved true. As we were taking the boats off their trailer hitches at the launch site, the sun was already burning off the mist. The cottonwoods, alders, and aspen all seemed to light up at once. The mountains were so far north and east of us that their views were entirely obscured by dense stands of lodgepole and fir.

The bottom of our driftboat scraped on the gravel and then came free and we were drifting along on the river. I looked into the water, at the ovoid stones of the riverbed. I could see a few pink salmon, humpbacks, exhausted from their spawning. Life was slowly ebbing out of these fish, and the salmon seemed to be awaiting the inevitable. I thought of the poem by Ted Hughes, "An August Salmon," where he describes a doomed cockfish, its strength unwinding like a spool in the river.

The color of the Bulkley was indeed different from what I had seen downstream the previous day. The sun poured down like honey on the river. The water reflected a forest and sky that seemed to be forever trading images in a changing, rippling display. I could see through the wavering clarity the river stones beneath the hull of our driftboat.

"I'm using the mirror of the timber to look into the water," Collin said. I stared into the upside-down reflection of black-and-green trees and I saw it, too, the river fluctuating between a mirror and a window that let me peer in on the bottom. I strained to notice steelhead-like shapes that might be down there amid the sunlit camouflage and refractions of cobble-stones and jumbled rock. Water plays tricks with reflections. Refraction makes what is deep appear shallow. The trees and sky reflected back in an endlessly changing, distorting mirror.

The river was only slightly tannic from a tea-stained runoff that came out of the forest. Despite the shifting and flickering, the ripples and reflections, I could see very clearly all the bottom contours, light and shadow at play on the river stones. The river appeared to be lapping up its own images.

Every now and again I'd spot a pink salmon barely moving, drifting with the current. These salmon were a gruesome sight, with white fungus and black discolorations on their backs. The males had developed prominent humpbacks.

"Most of the salmon have already spawned," Collin said. This wasn't a "pink year" up here, he explained, but pink salmon were plentiful nonetheless. In northern British Columbia, big runs of pinks come into the rivers in even-numbered, not odd-numbered years. In the southern part of the province, it's just the opposite. And yet the deformed carcasses littering the banks were a testament to the river's incredible fecundity.

"The river's running just a little high," Collin noted. "About a half-foot higher than normal for this time of year. We're just beginning to see steelhead."

The guides had the driftboats well spread-out on the river, so that the sports would hardly be aware at all of the presence of other angling parties. Collin kept a jetboat at the lodge, but today all his clients were sitting in oar-manned driftboats, which is Collin's preferred method of travel on his river. His intention is to disturb the serenity as little as possible. Mel and Cheryl

Edwards, a couple from California, accompanied me in Collin's driftboat. Cheryl was armed with a double-handed Spey rod, a lance so long it looked as if it could be used in a jousting tournament. Mel and I had single-handed rods. We were not fishing from the driftboat, however. As soon as Collin saw a likely place to fish, he would put us ashore.

John and Blee Orn were traveling in another driftboat. They were everyone's favorite couple at the lodge. They lived in Texas and were well into their retirement years. They would fish at their own sweet pace and relax on this trip, angling a little and watching the scenery slide by. John fished with a vintage bamboo fly rod. Their guide seemed to be having as much fun as they were.

With the morning sun high on the water, the cottonwoods, alders, and aspens were transforming the valley into a glorious orange-and-yellow stage. The slender aspen trees, which for some reason Canadians call poplars, burned the brightest colors of all. We seemed to pass by a number of likely steelhead drifts. The Walcott beat was a pastoral stretch along the upper river. There were no big rapids or whitewater thrills to speak of on this part of the river. Those were many miles farther downstream, in a remote wilderness section of the Bulkley called Driftwood Canyon. In all, the Bulkley flowed for seventy-six miles past forests, ranches, and small towns before reaching the Skeena. Beyond Driftwood Canyon, on past the town of Smithers, the Bulkley was flanked by three snowcapped mountain ranges: the Hazeltons to the north, the Babines to the east, and the Bulkleys, which formed the western barrier dividing the alpine plateau from the wet rain forests.

Collin maneuvered us onto the head of a long drift of water that looked quite suitable. I was out of the boat before the prow touched the gravel. Mel, Cheryl, and I had all put on dry flies at Collin's suggestion—he was that optimistic about our chances. Cheryl had recently learned how to cast her fourteen-foot, double-handed Spey rod, and she was really quite good at it. Her husband Mel and I would have to make do with the limitations of our single-hand rods.

When Collin saw me wading out well above my knees, he motioned me back a few feet toward the bank. He explained that the steelhead would be holding in the shallower water closer by the bank, and that I didn't want to be wading over them.

Collin had spread us out well apart from one another. We cast, intently following our floating flies in their arcs through their long drifts, sliding and skating the flies on the water. After each cast played out, we would step a few feet downstream and repeat the maneuver. This way we would get to cover all the likely water.

I held my rod high, tip pointing up, skating my dry fly over the water. I noticed that Mel held his rod tip almost to the water and seemed to be getting better drifts than I was. Cheryl was sliding her fly back and forth on the surface, getting some be-witching action out of the movement. I lowered my rod so that the tip was almost touching the river, and I found the results much more satisfying. I was able to make small mends, twitching and popping the fly a bit, creating a little more disturbance.

I peered into the water, looking for the camouflaged shapes of steelhead amid the river stones. Some years ago, I had stopped using polarized sunglasses while fishing on rivers. Po-larized glasses reduce the glare on the water and allow you to see the bottom clearly. It's much easier to spot fish that way. And fishermen are well advised to protect their eyes, as too much exposure to sunlight leads to cataracts. But I stopped wearing sunglasses a few years ago. I decided I wanted to see things as they really were. I wanted to see the world as it appears in real light. I figured what the hell, if we live long enough, we'll all get cataracts anyway.

We worked our way through the drift without getting any strikes or spotting any steelhead. So we climbed into the drift-boat and set off downstream. The shallower water near shore was like a lightly brewed tea full of golden sunlight. Aesthetics are a big part of the fishing experience. I like a river with a strong visual appeal. Especially a river with tall mountains and timbered banks. The Bulkley was meeting all my expectations.

Collin has nine weeks to make a living out of steelhead fish-ing on the Bulkley, so finding steelhead is a serious matter for him. His lodge caters to steelhead fishermen from the last week in August through the final week in October, the time when steelhead can be expected to be in the river. That isn't much of a window of opportunity.

"We have seen tremendous runs of steelhead in recent years," Collin told me. "For a steelhead river, this is a large river. Everything's just a little late and high this year. But I'm very optimistic."

Collin had every reason to be optimistic. The previous sea-son, the Bulkley—indeed, the entire Skeena system—had wit-nessed the largest ascension of steelhead in living memory.

Canada's Minister of Fisheries had ordered a drastic reduction of commercial netting of sockeye salmon at the mouth of the Skeena, and completely closed off the mouth during the coho salmon run. This reduced the so-called "incidental catch" of steelhead trapped in the salmon nets. The result was a banner year for sport fishermen. Just under seventy thousand steelhead swam up the Skeena River. Thirty thousand of them reached the Bulkley, with many continuing on into its headwater tributary, the Morice. And now everyone was anxious to see if this season would be a repeat of the previous year.

By midday, no one in our party had hooked a steelhead. So all the driftboats were put ashore for a streamside lunch. Collin carved a nut-brown loaf of home-baked bread and began to build turkey and roast beef sandwiches, while another guide heated up homemade vegetable soup. It was quite a festive affair, as streamside lunches tend to be. John and Blee sipped a little white wine out of plastic cups; later they would refresh themselves with a short nap before returning to their fishing.

We fished quite a number of good-looking steelhead runs that afternoon, but no one seemed to have any luck. Finally, as the afternoon was winding down and our fishing day was drawing to a close, Collin brought us to a spot on the river called Indian Summer. This would be our last shot at the steelhead. Collin warned us that the wading was very tricky here; the current was strong, and there was a jumble of rounded stones and boulders to slip on.

I fished at the head of the run; Mel and Cheryl were below me. The wading was indeed tough and the current strong. Collin directed me to cast well out toward a large sunken boulder that seemed to slow down the current. It would be a likely rest-ing place for a steelhead.

"There's a steelhead," Collin said suddenly. He was speak-ing to Mel, not to me. "It came right under your fly." He di-rected Mel to cast again to the same place. Mel made several more casts but nothing happened.

"All right, move down just a little and cast again," said Col-lin. Mel inched forward and hissed out another cast. This time when the steelhead rose, Mel struck too soon, snatching the fly away.

"That's okay," Collin said. "The steelhead on this river like to play with a fly. They'll keep coming back to it again and again." Collin said that once he had a steelhead come seventeen times to his dry fly. Collin told us that he kept snatching the fly away from the fish, playing with it, just to see how many times it would rise. Collin directed Mel to step downstream a foot or so and try again.

"Now!" Collin said. Mel came up tight on the fish, and his rod began to quiver and jerk up and down. The fish pulled off line, trying to move downstream. Mel held fast, planting him-self in position. If the steelhead decided to make a line-smoking run, Mel would have a tough time following it downstream over the slippery rocks. The steelhead twisted and turned under-water, but made no jumps. Mel's rod vibrated, dipping up and down. He was getting a good fight out of the steelhead, and he appeared to be in control, when suddenly his rod snapped back, lifeless. The steelhead had thrown the hook, leaving Mel staring into the void where his fish had been.

"What did I do wrong?" Mel asked with a rueful laugh.

"Nothing," said Collin. "Sometimes they just come off."

The next morning I was driving on the dirt logging road that follows the Morice River. It was evident to me from the moment I first laid eyes on them that the Morice and Bulkley were one and the same river. They supposedly join one another near the tiny town of Houston, but this confluence is a mapmaker's trick. There is a skinny stream, a river in name only, that comes into the larger river near the hamlet, and this is called the upper Bulkley River, barely a little more than a creek joining the main river. This narrow tributary stream originates to the east at Bulkley Lake. Both river and lake were named after a colonel in the United States Army, Charles Bulkley, who was chief construction engineer of a wilderness telegraph wire that had been raised here in the 1860s to carry the first telegraph line up into the Yukon, the Collins Overland Telegraph Trail. The wire is long gone, but the Telegraph Trail still exists, chronicled in Edward Hoagland's *Notes From the Century Before*. The larger stream, the Morice River, flows out of Morice Lake, and these two bodies of water had been named in the mid-nineteenth century by Father Morice, a missionary turned explorer and cartographer. But the Morice abruptly ends at Houston where it becomes the Bulkley. Father Morice was quite bitter after the provincial government decided to name all the water flowing below the town of Houston after the colonel. The cleric believed the glory should have been his.

The big river, the Morice/Bulkley, or whatever you want to

call it, comes directly out of Morice Lake, a liquid gem surrounded on three sides by mountains. Because the Morice River drains a catch-basin lake rather than a mountain glacier, it is one of the last rivers to discolor after a rain and the first to come back into shape. This makes the Morice an ideal stream for fly-fishing. The Morice gets an early run of comparatively smaller steelhead in late August and early September. They move up the Bulkley rather quickly and settle into the Morice. The Morice fish are a separate race of steelhead from the ones that will later settle into holding positions downstream in the Bulkley. These early Morice River steelhead are mainly does averaging five to seven pounds. These females will be joined later in the season by much larger bucks, some weighing up to fifteen pounds. Because Morice steelhead arrive earlier in the season, steelhead fishermen in the Bulkley Valley usually begin their season on the Morice. And whenever the fishing is slow on the Bulkley, a fisherman can usually get some action on the Morice.

The autumn morning was of such brilliance that the blue river looked startling against a yellow-and-orange blaze of aspens. Although a dirt road followed the length of the Morice, I found there was little access to the stream except at a few obviously-marked turnoffs along the logging road. Bushwhacking fishermen have been known to blaze their own trails down to the river in order to get away from other anglers. I drove most of the length of the logging road in order to get a good look at the river valley. The flame-colored aspens, or poplars, lit up the valley like bonfires.

Coming round a bend, I spotted a huge expanse of hills on

the far side of the river that were covered in groves of brand-new quaking aspen growing at the feet of dead spruce trees. The aspens were nowhere near their full height; they appeared quite tiny next to the spruce trunks. This was a sure sign there had been a recent fire. I pulled over to look at the scene. An informational plaque set up alongside the logging road informed me that I was looking at the spot of the so-called Swiss Fire. A few years back, some fellows from Switzerland who were in the woods smoking salmon, accidentally set the forest ablaze, burning sixty thousand acres.

Aspens spring up quickly over moist, fire-cleared ground. Within the shelter of these quaking groves, in time taller and longer-lived conifers would grow, eventually shading out and eliminating the aspens. Aspens grow quickly because of the means by which they gather solar energy. Unlike the leaves of most trees, aspen leaves produce chlorophyll on both sides, enabling the trees to use the energy of the sun to manufacture food more efficiently. Because aspen leafstalks are flat, the leaves turn from side to side in only the slightest change of breeze, exposing both sides of the leaf to sunlight. The constant rustling sound gives rise to their popular name, quaking aspen.

The aspens in the hills above the Morice were simply resplendent. The green chlorophyll factory in the leaves had closed down with the autumn weather, allowing the natural pigments of orange and yellow to shine through. This orange-and-yellow melodrama would play itself out until the cold winds of an advancing autumn stripped the aspens bare.

More than anything, I appreciated the fact that the Morice flowed through protected forest land. I saw no houses or settlements along the bank. This was a wild river, the kind of experience I was looking for in British Columbia.

I drove back downriver until I came to a parking turnoff where a bridge crossed the river. It was perhaps too obvious a spot, but I chose it anyway. Throwing on my waders and assembling my gear, I scrambled down the high bank. My plan was to walk as far upstream as I could, and fish my way back.

The Morice River had a beautiful blue tint that showed itself in the sunshine. An island close by the shore split the river, creating an interesting side channel. On my way back, I could fish that side channel and then cross over to the island and explore the far shore there. That would double the amount of shoreline that I could fish.

As I walked along the riverbank, I caught the occasional whiff of dead salmon. The air was so clean and fresh that the rare pocket of stench hardly seemed to matter. When I got well enough upstream, I waded out, careful not to go any deeper than my knees. I would have to take care not to hang any backcasts in the trees along the bank.

I spent the next half hour fishing, casting in a leisurely rhythm and taking short steps downstream. Nothing much happened. And then I chanced a glance behind me and I beheld the most real thing I had ever seen: a black bear, not many yards away. It was on the very path I had been walking earlier. The bear was breakfasting on a dead salmon. Twice it looked up from its meal to watch me watching it. I was stuck in midstream; there was no place for me to retreat. Believe me, seeing a bear in a photograph isn't the same thing as seeing one up close in the wild. It was utterly unnerving. The bear's coat was exceptionally black and shiny. Clearly this was a healthy, well-fed bear.

The only thing to do was to turn around and keep on fishing. Black bears are a problem only if you stumble upon one accidentally and scare it. Or if you get between a sow and her cubs. I was well aware that my chances of being killed by a bear in the woods were actually less than my chances of being killed by one of my fellow human beings. But I am one of the few people who has actually known someone who was killed by a bear.

Readers may recall an incident that took place a few years ago where a man was killed while backpacking in Gates of the Arctic National Park in Alaska. The man accidentally stumbled upon and startled a giant Alaskan brown bear. The bear attacked and killed him. Authorities say the man died instantly, although how they could determine this to a certainty was beyond me. In any case I hope it was true and that his suffering was minimal. That fellow's name was Rob Bell, and as young men the two of us had worked together as reporters on the same newspaper in one of the mid-Atlantic seaboard states. Rob went on to take a law degree and he joined a firm specializing in labor-rights issues. He loved the outdoors, was an experienced backpacker, and presumably he knew how to conduct himself in bear country—which means tomorrow is promised to no one.

Alaskan brown bears grow even larger than the North American grizzlies of the Rocky Mountain West. They grow to such a tremendous size because of their diet of salmon, which is rich in fat. The great majority of British Columbian grizzlies inhabit the rain forests closer to the coast. But there are grizzlies up here on the Morice, too, and it is necessary to stay alert while fishing.

I looked behind me and saw the bear had left. No doubt the animal had moved off to scare up another salmon carcass. See, nothing to worry about at all. Bears embody the dread that comes with any true appreciation of the apartness, the otherness, in nature. The word *awe* comes from the Middle English *aghe*, which means "to be afraid." Awe is a mixture of reverence, fear, and wonder caused by something majestic, sublime, or sacred. Bears fill me with awe. They have the power to inspire both fear and fearful reverence.

What I really hoped to see sometime during my trip was one of the unusual white bears the Indians of British Columbia call the spirit bear. Spirit bears are actually black bears with white fur, the result of the mating of two black bears with a double-recessive gene. The recessive gene shows up in the black bears of British Columbia about as often as red hair does in people. One cub born to a litter might be black, another a creamy white. The spirit bear is also called a kermode, or kermodie, after Dr. Francis Kermode, who classified *Ursus americanus kermodie* as a subspecies of black bear in 1905. Spirit bears are much smaller than polar bears, and a little darker, too, something like the color of dirty snow. The Indians have a special regard for the kermodie, seeing them as living reminders of past ice ages. Tsimshian legend has it that spirit bears can assume human form.

I waded slowly downstream, carefully working all the water I could reach with my casts. There wasn't another angler anywhere in my vicinity. I had this lovely stretch of river to myself. I crossed the stream at the place where the island divided the channel, and worked the far shoreline. Then I recrossed, fishing my way down the side channel from the forest bank. No strikes, no signs of fish.

Finally I came opposite the lee of the island. The best water lay directly below me, where the main and side channels both converged at the bottom of the island to scoop out a deep hole in the river. I knew instinctively that there would be a steelhead hiding in that hole.

I skated my dry fly across the deeper water where the two currents met. My fly stopped suddenly, and was sucked down in a swirl. I felt a heavy weight pulling on my line. I struck and the rod came alive in my hand, bucking and pulsing. The jolt of a large steelhead ran up the rod and into my arm.

The steelhead leapt in a flash of silver that reflected the sunlight, and crashed back into the river. Line ran off my reel in a ratcheting complaint. Fishermen who spend a lot of time on the Morice talk about steelhead that run like Caribbean bonefish, steelhead they call "Morice crazies."

My steelhead jumped three more times in a shower of droplets, and was well below me before I had the presence of mind to palm the reel and check the steelhead flight. To my horror I saw that my reel was now seriously backlashed. This is the one complaint I have with these neat old Hardy click drags. Reels that don't have sophisticated drag systems sometimes allow their spool to whip around faster than the line can be pulled off by a fish. The result is a bird's nest in the arbor. Nervous moments passed as I freed the tangle of backlash from my Hardy, somehow managing to hold the fish in place at the same time. And then the line was free and I felt the fish running again. The steelhead was strong and heavy and full of fight, and the hookup felt solid. I somehow knew at that moment that I was going to land my first British Columbia steelhead. And what a way to take him, on a dry fly!

I regained line, pumping and pulling, and keeping a steady pressure on the fish. Eventually I had it thrashing around on the surface. My rod bent dangerously. But I guided the kicking steelhead toward the shallow water near shore where I could tail him. Once, when it saw me, the big fish panicked and bolted, taking away more line; but I managed to bring him back. By now the fish was too exhausted to fight any longer. I drew the fish toward me, forcing its head out of the water with my rod raised high above my own head.

It was an enormous fish, the largest summer steelhead I had ever caught. A thick band of red ran down its silver side. This was one of the hefty Morice River bucks. The fish must have weighed thirteen pounds. Magnificent.

I removed the hook from the jaw and rocked the steelhead gently back and forth in the current to revive it. I allowed water to pass through its gills, giving the fish time to regain oxygen and recover its equilibrium. The last thing I wanted was for this magnificent fish to go into toxic shock and die from a buildup of lactic acid. All steelhead on the Morice must be released unharmed; all steelhead must be released on any river in the Skeena system. Those are the rules. Regardless of any fishing regulation, there was no way I would have made myself kill this wonderful animal.

This was great. My first Canadian steelhead, and on a dry fly, too. This was why I had come to British Columbia. I cradled in my arms a wild animal no less spectacular than an eagle or a bear. No wonder I felt such exhilaration. Awesome.

RIVERS OF MIST

WHERE THE BULKLEY and Skeena Rivers met, I entered a region of mist and deep gorges. The Skeena is known as the "river of mists," and as those mists lifted I began to see the snowpacked peaks of great mountain ranges all around me. The Skeena appeared as a slow but powerful slate-gray stream sliding under a sky the color of smoke.

'Ksan means "between the banks." At the tiny community of Hazelton, where the Bulkley and Skeena Rivers come together under cottonwood trees in the shadow of Mount Rocher Deboule, I saw the communal lodges and carving house of 'Ksan Indian Village, a replicate Tsimshian village built in the 1960s. Hazelton had once gone by its Indian name, Gitanmax—"where the people fish by torchlight." The Gitksan are renowned totem carvers. Their elaborate cedar poles tell family legends and tribal history in the form of mythopoeic animal and spirit dramas. When a totem pole goes up, everyone knows who it belongs to and what story the artist was telling, and why the artist felt compelled to tell it. A totem could be anywhere from six to a hundred feet in height. An artist might carve fifty in a lifetime. But even the oldest poles standing have been around for only a little more than a century. The totems can't last because of the wet air of the Pacific Northwest, which rots the wood. The survival of the art form as well as the actual artifact depends upon each new generation of carvers taking up the craft.

The road to the Kispiox River led me across two of the most stunning gorges I had ever stared down into. *Kispiox* means "the place of the hiding people." At the Gitksan village of Kispiox, I counted fifteen totems pointing at the sky, more iconography revealed in the shapes of ravens, bears, and porcupines. Close by here, the Kispiox River empties into the Skeena.

Two British Columbia rivers, the Kispiox and Babine, regularly yield the world's largest steelhead. Evidently size is hereditary, for certain waters produce races of giants, while others nearby might not. The Babine—just a mountain range over—is a wilderness river, much harder to reach than the Kispiox, which drains a fertile valley with a lower gradient. Some anglers will visit British Columbia and fish only the Kispiox during their stay, so intent are they on bagging a steelhead over twenty-five pounds, or getting their names in the record books, or winning contests. Just as every artist longs to create at least one indisputable masterpiece, so, too, does a true fisherman long to catch one for the record books. American steelheaders have been trekking to British Columbia since the mid-1950s, after *Field & Stream* magazine first published the results of its annual big-fish contest. It seemed that the records for lure and fly-caught steelhead all came out of a then little-known river called the Kispiox. One of those anglers who pulled his trailer up to the Skeena country every autumn was Karl Mausser of Los Angeles, California, who in 1962 landed a thirty-three pounder on the Kispiox, the largest steelhead ever caught on a fly rod, a record that officially has gone unbroken to this day. Unofficially, the record has been broken many times since then by fly-fishermen who have released larger steelhead, some up to thirty-seven pounds. But those are unofficial records. Karl Mausser was an interesting fellow who would camp for months beside the rivers, subsisting on steelhead, mushrooms, berries, and whatever else he could forage out of the woods. Karl was said to have some regrets about killing that trophy because it brought so much publicity to the Kispiox. He never killed another steelhead after 1978, converting to the philosophy of catch-and-release. He never missed a season in British Columbia, either, and he continued to fish well into his eighties. Last I heard, he was still alive and doing well in Los Angeles. Fly-fishermen have been coming to the Kispiox hoping to repeat Karl's performance ever since. They begin arriving in September, and many stay on right through October and even into November, as chill rains turn to snow and fly lines ice up inside the rod guides.

A soft drizzle fell as I drove through the mixed farm- and forestland of the Kispiox Valley. I spied coverts that probably hid ruffed grouse, which locals up here call willow grouse. No doubt the woods were full of bears that stayed fat not only on river salmon but by raiding the oat fields and potato patches on nearby farms. Every now and again I'd get a glimpse of the river through thick willows and brush lining the banks.

The Kispiox was a dark river, containing a fair amount of

tannin, a tea-stained runoff from the forest. These forest leach-
ings had made the Kispiox a much browner river than the bluer
snowmelt tones of the Bulkley and Skeena. The steelhead in
the river were darker, too. In late autumn, steelhead in the Kispiox, particularly the males, displayed more reds and olives
than fish in the Bulkley and Skeena, which tended to be
brighter. Steelhead have color receptors in their skin that are
light-sensitive and so they tend to mimic their river back-
grounds. If you were to take a Kispiox fish and put it in the
Bulkley, it would be only a matter of minutes before it would
brighten up.

Kispiox steelhead differed from fish in their sister rivers in
several other significant ways. For one, Kispiox steelhead didn't
seem particularly inclined to rise to dry flies. This probably had
something to do with the river's browner color, its opacity and
limited visibility. At its best the Kispiox is always a little murky.
The Kispiox doesn't originate in a catch-basin lake, as the Morice and Babine do. Rivers coming out of lakes seem to stay
clearer longer, even after it rains. But a river like the Kispiox
tended to be less stable. Heavy rains can knock out the Kispiox
for days. Even in clear weather, melting snow from high on the
mountains draining into the forests can keep the Kispiox high
and discolored.

It's a given that in any stream, most salmon and steelhead
will be spotted resting very near the bottom. A fish on the bottom is looking up from relative darkness into relative brightness. And so when rivers are high or discolored, an angler has
a much better chance of catching salmonids when he gets his
fly down deep, where it can be seen, and this often takes a

sinking line. On the Kispiox, a river that carries a lot of color and tends to be more opaque than other streams, sinking lines, or sink-tips, are considered the way to go. Also, the very largest fish in any river system are the ones least likely to move up from the bottom to chase a surface fly; and fly-fishermen come to the Kispiox specifically seeking trophy steelhead.

In autumn, steelhead start coming into the Kispiox by the time most of the salmon have died. This fall, like the salmon, the steelhead were just a little late showing up. Fishing had been slow, just as on the Bulkley. But fishermen said the river was just beginning to pick up.

I stopped at River's Edge Campground to buy my permit. Several well-maintained trails led down to the river. The Bear Hole, the spot where Karl Mausser caught his world-record steelhead, was accessible from the campground, and, I figured, why not go for the glory.

The pools around the campground were well defined, and I found the wading from the bank fairly simple. The current speed was much to my liking. On steelhead streams, runs that are likely to hold steelhead are called drifts. Steelhead seek out reliable holding places as they move upstream. The exact spots they choose are usually determined by the bottom contours, the depth of the river, and the current speed. As steelhead move upstream, they are replaced by new steelhead that occupy the very same spots. Year after year, barring natural changes in the river, returning steelhead tend to occupy the same positions in a stream. It is as if the fish have somehow inherited from their ancestors an interior memory of their home river. New fish keep coming back to the same old places.

I entered the river one pool above the Bear Hole and fished my way slowly and methodically downstream. I had put on a Teeny 300-grain line, shortened my leader, and tied on a large, heavy fly known as an Egg-Sucking Leech (or, jocularly, a Lawyer Fly). The purpose for this heavy ordnance was to get my offering down deep, where I believed the steelhead would prefer it. Bottom-dredging is not my favorite way to catch a fish, and it seemed a pity to do it on a beautiful autumn steelhead river. But when in Rome . . .

I varied the direction of my casts, depending on the water flow. Where the water was swift, I directed the cast slightly upstream and mended (or mended as much as is humanly possible with a sink-tip) in order to keep both my line and my fly deep and to prevent them from being pushed upward by the current. But most of my drifts called for simple casts straight across the river, followed by a quick mend to slow down the speed of the fly.

I followed the progress of my sunken line as the fly ticked along the bottom, catching itself on river stones. I'd pull up on the rod, thinking I had a strike, only to find myself hung up on the bottom. The 300-grain shooter was simply too heavy for this water. It was one thing to be able to feel every little tremor and hesitant vibration; another to be hanging up on every third or fourth cast.

I found that I could only keep the fly moving by stripping a little line and fishing with a slight retrieve. That would be fine if I were fishing for coho salmon, which respond well to a retrieved fly. But in steelhead fishing, it's generally better to fish without any retrieve at all, letting the fly swing along at the speed of the current. A retrieved fly can scare a steelhead and discourage it from striking.

I was in an untenable position. I was fishing the fly too fast; but if I slowed down I'd hang up on the bottom. And I couldn't mend the line effectively with a 300-grain sinking line. I needed a slower, intermediate line, something halfway between what I was using and a floating line. But I didn't have one. Fly lines cost fifty to sixty dollars apiece, a lot of money for what is little more than plastic-coated clothesline. No doubt about it, the fly-fishing industry had me by the short hairs.

Half the pleasure in fly-fishing is in the casting. But this was hardly the kind of fly casting that makes you go all cosmic. The 300-grain line was simply too heavy to be any fun. So in frustration I switched over to my floating line. I figured this would pretty much take me out of the ball game as far as the bottom-loving steelhead of the Kispiox were concerned. But a floater is a pleasure to cast, and it mends beautifully, making it much easier to control the fly. There's simply more poetry in it.

By repeatedly mending, I was able to keep my fly maybe a foot below the surface throughout the best parts of the drift; but I could do little to keep the fly from rising to the surface as the cast played itself out and the line finished its swing below me. I only hoped that a steelhead would be in the mood to move off the bottom and chase it that far.

I felt my fly catch on to something soft and yielding, like a branch. When I drew up on the rod to free the line, I could feel the branch trembling in the current. And then the branch began swimming away downstream. At first I thought I had dislodged the branch from the river bottom and that the current was sweeping it away downstream. But then the branch changed directions on me. It was pulling line sideways through the current.

I couldn't believe it—I had hooked a steelhead. I tightened up on the line to set the hook, and the fish, now annoyed, began to pull away with greater determination. I struck hard with the rod and this caused the steelhead to respond with a sharp tug of its own. Now the line was leaving my reel in a slow but steady buzz. The fish had finally been aroused.

The steelhead rose to the surface, splashed around for a little bit, and then sounded, trying to pull away underwater. I held it steady in the current, keeping pressure on the rod. This wasn't anything even like the kind of fight I had gotten from that steelhead on the Morice. Not once did this steelhead jump or flip into the air. My fish continued its steady effort to resist the upward pull of my line and leader. Slowly, I was able to draw it toward the bank.

I applied all the pressure I thought the monofilament leader could bear, and the steelhead's resistance faltered. I could feel the near-deadweight of the fish. By now I was fighting more current than fish. Holding the rod high, I lifted the steelhead's head out of the water and led it into the sandy shallows of a cove that had formed next to the bank. When it saw me, the steelhead panicked for the first time, and began splashing around real hard; but it lacked the strength to make a burning run. Within minutes I had the exhausted fish beside me, and I was reaching down to release the hook from the corner of its jaw.

It was a beautiful henfish, what the British Columbians call a doe, with a silver sheen and a faint blush of rose and lavender on her sides and gill plates. I freed the hook and revived the steelhead. With an almost invisible shudder, she was gone.

I couldn't get over the gentleness and subtlety of the initial hookup. It was nothing like the savage take of the steelhead I had hooked the previous day on the Morice. This was more like one of those soft tugs that I had become accustomed to while fishing icy winter steelhead streams in California. More like a tap than a yank.

Well, at least I knew that a Kispiox steelhead could be taken on a floating line. I didn't want to draw any sweeping generalizations on the basis of catching just one fish. But Kispiox steelhead, known to be among the biggest steelhead in British Columbia, are not known as the toughest scrappers. At least not by the time they reach the Kispiox. If Bulkley and Morice steelhead are more responsive to surface flies and tend to be more aggressive fighters, that is more likely a result of their habitat. The Kispiox by its nature is a different river, with a slower gradient, and it stays slightly colder on average than its sister rivers. All of these things can affect a steelhead's metabolism and reflexes.

The huge Kispiox steelhead first have to pass up through the lower Skeena, and many local fly-fishermen make a point of fishing for the big Kispiox brutes while those fish are still in the Skeena and have more steam. This was something visiting anglers were only just beginning to catch on to. The trick was in locating the big fish in the great expanse of the huge Skeena River. Local fly-fishermen were making it a custom to hit the gravel banks of the Skeena just above and below the town of Terrace, or upriver around Kitwanga, starting in August and early September. That way they could catch bright Kispiox steelhead so fresh they still had sea lice on them. It was mid-September, and the steelhead were only just arriving in the Kispiox, so there would be many sea-bright Kispiox-bound fish still out there in the Skeena.

The Sportsman's Kispiox Lodge was the kind of place that made you feel you were coming home even when you had never been there before. Everything about it said steelhead. Waders hung on pegs in the foyer and boots had been left to dry before the fireplace. I was careful to wipe my boots so I wouldn't track up the carpet. The leaf-strewn grounds were soggy with rain and there was mud and water everywhere.

I walked down a hallway past the bedrooms and came out onto the dining room. Just off the dining room, a darkly paneled wall was covered in woodblock prints displaying photographic portraits of old-timers in the Kispiox Valley. Maybe it was the photographer's art or something, but the love these elderly couples showed for one another just poured out of the portraits. This contributed to the rustic, comfortable, homey feeling inside the lodge.

I hadn't been here five minutes, and already I was feeling nostalgic about the place. "Nostalgia" is an abused term, often confused with sentimentality, but it literally means "to return." This can be anything from an overwhelming longing to return home, to a longing for one's hometown or homeland, or a yearning for something far away and long ago, or simply a desire to return to a happier time. To me the lodge meant that kind of happiness.

The lodge was built in 1966 by Gary Wookey, a member of a very prominent pioneer family in the valley. In his book on British Columbia, Edward Hoagland referred to the Wookeys as a local version of the Snopses. Ravenswood Campground on the Kispiox, once known as Wookey's Resort, used to be the Wookey family farm. Gary Wookey's lodge began as a simple roadside stand where customers sat on spruce stumps before a plank counter. When his tiny luncheonette burned to the ground, Gary moved his operation up the hill a little ways from the road, and put in a kitchen, grill, counter, and a few guest rooms. In time, his simple, single-story lodge became popular with steelhead fishermen who were looking for some place cozier to stay than in a campground. Over time the lodge became so popular that separate cabins were added.

In the 1970s, Wookey's lodge was purchased by Margaret Clay, a friendly, no-nonsense woman who is the patriarch of another family that was to become prominent in the valley. There is a simplicity and an implied competence in the people who live and work in British Columbia, something one expects from people who live in a place where only the hardy and self-sufficient can make do. Margaret Clay personifies all that. Margaret ran the lodge throughout the seventies, with her children helping her. The Sportsman's Kispiox Lodge was definitely a family affair. The lodge wasn't one of those fantasy steelhead resorts for well-heeled anglers. Rather it was built for simple comfort, and it had a distinctly rustic flavor. During fishing season, the staff worked eighteen-hour days. Meals at the lodge were hearty rather than gourmet, designed to stoke anglers with enough calories to get them through a long, cold day of steelhead fishing.

Margaret sold the lodge in 1980, but she decided to buy it back in 1992. Now she had plans to retire once again and sell the lodge to Allan Larson, a farmer who lived up in the northern end of the valley, a place where the electrical power still had a habit of frequently going out in bad weather. Larson told me his own plans were to renovate the lodge, add a few more modern amenities, and expand his season to accommodate rafters, hunters, and cross-country skiers who vacationed in the valley.

On my first night at the lodge, I met Margaret's grandson, Aaron Wadley, a young fishing guide. Outdoor guides have an enormous amount of knowledge about the natural order of things. I have yet to come across a guide who wasn't at heart a naturalist and a crusading environmentalist. For Aaron, guiding is a family business. Aaron's uncle, Gordon Wadley, runs an outfit called Kispiox River Tours, and he and his nephew take anglers on float trips on the Kispiox and other nearby waters. Many of Gordon's sports stay at the lodge.

Aaron works with the Kispiox Watershed Protection Coalition, a conservation organization devoted to protecting the river valley. Aaron and I sat at the bar in the lounge, as members of a local rock band set up drums and amplifiers behind us. I asked Aaron if the band wouldn't bother the fishermen, who were known for going to bed early.

"The lodge is soundproofed," Aaron explained. "The music won't bother them." The lodge was a center of entertainment in the valley. Locals came to eat dinner in the restaurant, and on weekends they showed up to enjoy rock and roll.

Aaron unrolled a poster-size photo across the bar. It was a satellite photograph taken of the Kispiox Valley from outer space. I was looking down at the river valley, the backside of its drainage, a portion of the Babine river to the east, and on the west, the Kitwangcool drainage. The satellite photo looked like a Jackson Pollock painting, and had cost almost as much. The Kispiox Watershed Coalition had purchased it from the B.C. Ministry of Forests. The outer-space photograph told the story of the Kispiox River from an environmental standpoint. The blue splotches I saw were glaciers and snow peaks. Light-orange and tan colors depicted alpine terrain. Darker oranges showed the effects of clear-cutting. Pitch-black patches indicated virgin forests, and the gray was agriculture. There wasn't as much solid black as I had expected, and there was far too much dark orange. This chunk of British Columbia was not as spotless as one might at first suppose.

"You can see that the logging roads are now pressing into the Babine," Aaron said. The healthiest forests, those solid-black colors in the satellite photo, were concentrated along the Babine watershed. I got a clear idea of what was in store for them.

In British Columbia, about a thousand square miles of ancient forest gets chopped annually. Timber companies have carved out clear-cuts as large as 180 square miles in size in some portions of the province. Researchers at the University of British Columbia have estimated that all the old-growth forest presently not under some form of protection will be gone within two decades. Only about five or ten percent of the forest land is protected by parks and other preserves. Naturally, most of the valuable timber comes out of the thick coastal forests that provide critical habitat for salmon and steelhead. All this rapine was taking place in a province whose official motto is *Splendor sine occasu* ("Splendour without diminishment").

Northern B.C. hadn't yet been hit as hard as the southern and central portions of the province. In the farthest reaches of the rugged coastal mountains, old-growth was tougher to get at and the timber more expensive to take out. Trackless expanses of forest still protected more remote riverine habitat. In this part of British Columbia, it was as if the clocks had been turned back fifty years. But it wasn't going to stay that way forever. In the fullness of time, the trees would lose.

One only had to look at the southern and central portions of the province to see the devastation that was coming. Logging along southern rivers had taken a dreadful toll. Once foresters cut and replanted, but B.C. was now thirty years behind in the replanting. Hurt most were the rivers close by population centers in the city of Vancouver, in the southwestern corner of B.C., and on overcrowded Vancouver Island. Hundreds of smaller breeding populations of salmon and steelhead already had been exterminated; more than six hundred existing runs were presently at risk. And in eastern B.C. all the salmon and steelhead populations that once had thrived in the Columbia headwaters were now extinct, thanks to my fellow countrymen and the dams we had built on the Columbia River downstream in the United States.

I asked Aaron if there were any undiscovered steelhead rivers in British Columbia. Secret rivers that were little-known and unexplored, perhaps in roadless areas to the north. Places where fishermen could go after all the known wild places had been exhausted. Aaron said that almost all the runoff from rivers north of the Babine on the eastern side of the Skeena came off snow and ice fields, and so the streams were regarded as too murky to be of much interest to fly-fishermen.

But a few seasons ago, Aaron and a few of his friends had arranged to be dropped by helicopter onto a gravel bank on the remote Sicintine River to see what could be found in the way of sport. The Sicintine drains into the upper Skeena. In summertime, when the ice fields are melting, there's a lot of runoff and the Sicintine runs dirty.

"But we went up there in early November," Aaron told me. "It was almost like winter camping. Everything was pretty much frozen up. The river was throwing ice. There was some anchor ice developing on the rocks of the riverbed, and some flush ice on the surface. I think because of that, we didn't see many fish. The only fish we saw were the ones sunning themselves in the shallow water. There were four of us fishing, and we managed to hook only one fish on a four-day trip."

The Sicintine is about half the size of the Kispiox, and it flows through a rugged, beautiful valley. Aaron said the average depth was only about four feet, which made it ideal for wading.

"You have a lot of flat runs," Aaron said, "and then you start getting into canyon-type water with big holding tanks, where you aren't able to see all the way down into the water. It's a neat place. But they're starting to put logging roads in there.

They've developed some cutblocks in the area, and I imagine soon we'll have road access, which is unfortunate."

Aaron said that most of his fishing is centered around his home base on the Kispiox. I asked him how the current season was progressing. Aaron said everyone had great expectations because the previous season had been so bountiful. Returns of steelhead had been so great the previous year that people were even talking about rewriting the regulations to allow local anglers—that is, those who made their homes in the province—to keep a steelhead legally. But Aaron thought that was jumping the gun.

"I think it's a bit too early for that," he said. "Everybody talks about this being a giant year coming up, but we'll have to wait and see. Last year was phenomenal, though. It was like winning the lottery."

Up early the next morning, I walked into a dining room already packed with steelhead anglers eating breakfast. The room rang with the clatter and rattle of tableware. Margaret's sister Betty was laying out box lunches on the kitchen counter. These were for fishermen who would be going out on all-day float trips. Permits were being filled in for the river floats. Gordon Wadley, his nephew Aaron, and half a dozen other guides were huddled together in the kitchen, drinking coffee and plotting out the morning's itinerary. Outside, there was a light drizzle in the air, but Gordon said the river was actually running slightly clearer than it had been on the previous day. Betty set a plate of eggs Benedict before me. Margaret Clay, who was supervising the scene, looked over at me and said, "It's like getting children off to school in the morning."

Because the fishing was so slow on the Kispiox, I decided I would fish the Suskwa River. The Suskwa is a tributary of the lower Bulkley River; it is not all that far from the Kispiox, and it is said to be the river where the guides go fishing on their days off. The Suskwa was small by the standards of the Skeena system. But the river had some very large steelhead in it. And because commercial river floats weren't allowed, the Suskwa got relatively little fishing pressure.

It was evident that the drainage had been heavily logged. I managed to find a dirt logging road that led me deep into the woods, and this took me to an old wooden bridge spanning the river. The timber boards shook and rumbled as my car crossed the span. On my way in I had kicked up so much dust that my car license plates were entirely obscured.

Although the drizzle had let up, the morning was still quite overcast, and this made it ideal for steelhead fishing. Less light on the water is a good thing, as steelhead don't seem to respond well under bright conditions. They are looking up from darkness into light, and with sunshine directly on the water, it can be difficult for a steelhead to see a fly.

I found a place to park close by the bridge, and assembled my gear. I decided to head downstream first, where a woody island split the river neatly in half. The channel nearest me looked like a flawless steelhead drift. It was only a good cast across to the island and I could cover every inch of the water. I started at the head of the pool, with a dry fly.

I couldn't have asked for a more scenic backdrop for my

fishing. The river flowed in the direction of distant, glacier-topped mountains. In moments when the sun slipped out from behind the clouds, the snow and ice on those peaks shined like hammered tin. The parting clouds were like a rising stage curtain on a play about nature.

I had in my fly box about a dozen old salmon flies. These were trout flies, really, left over from my days fishing the Madison River in Montana more than a decade ago.

These "salmon flies" were actually imitations of big stoneflies that are used in trout fishing on Rocky Mountain trout rivers such as the Madison during the famous "salmon fly" hatch, when large trout rise to gobble egg-laying stoneflies. These salmon flies were shaped very much like the flies being sold by the gross to steelhead fly-fishermen in the shop at Smithers at three and four bucks a pop. More crackpot theories have been expounded on what kind of flies will catch fish than on any other aspect of our sport. Fly patterns are entirely irrelevant in salmon and steelhead fishing. A salmon or a steelhead will attack just about anything that is tied onto a hook. That's if the fish is in a mood to bite in the first place. When the water is high, large flies are preferable; when low and clear, the flies should be smaller. That's really all anyone needs to know.

Fishing a so-called dry fly in steelhead fishing can mean one of two things. It can refer to a fly that is "dead-drifted," meaning that it floats on the surface without any line tension. But it usually refers to a technique that involves skating or sliding a floating fly across the surface under tension so that the fly creates a visible wake. The skittering fly and V-shaped wake catches the attention of a resting steelhead. The angler casts directly across or slightly below him and brings the fly down and across the current. By maintaining just the right amount of tension on the line, the fly begins to skim the water while remaining upright on the surface. The sight of a fly moving in this fashion sometimes triggers a very aggressive response in a steelhead.

I have always thought that fishing a waking fly on the surface would be a more effective method of catching steelhead than fishing a fly wet, although the opposite is taken to be true. Wet flies fished on floating lines travel only a few inches under the surface of the river. In effect, a steelhead has just about as far to travel up from the bottom to grab the fly. Because of the wake kicked up on the surface, you would think that a skated fly would be even more visible to a steelhead. And yet getting a steelhead to rise to a dry fly is considered the apex of the sport, a more impressive achievement than tricking a steelhead into striking a sunken fly. Certainly it is the most thrilling moment in fly-fishing. A skated fly provokes a particularly violent and showy rise out of a steelhead.

I cast straight across at 90 degrees, so that the first part of my drift was drag-free, but then the greater portion came under tension and soon the fly was swinging and skating and kicking up a wake. By the time I had waded two-thirds of the way down the pool, a fish swirled at my waking fly, bumped it, and disappeared. I struck, but pulled back on nothing.

It is not uncommon for an individual steelhead to make several rises to a fly before actually taking it. That's what Collin Schadrech had been talking about back there on the Bulkley.

No one knows for sure why steelhead do this. No one knows why steelhead take flies at all, for that matter. Fish have no brains to speak of, but they do have a remarkable collection of reflexes. Aggression, territorial response, behavior that we might call "curiosity" or "playfulnes"—even feeding, which is the most obvious explanation of all—no one can say for certain what is going on here.

Many fishermen believe that salmon and steelhead take flies out of territorial or defensive responses. But steelhead and salmon are more apt to take flies sooner after coming into a river than later, and it is later that they have the most need to defend their turf. When the actual spawning starts to get under way, and the need to repel invaders becomes most acute—say, when smolts are attempting to dart in and fertilize the females— the big fish, males and females, can hardly be induced into attacking flies, so intent are they on having sex. On the few occasions where I was so rude as to fish over paired and mating steelhead, my attempts at coitus interruptus all failed. The fish were completely oblivious of my fly.

I suspect that a steelhead's strike is more a latent feeding response than anything else. Now I know that a steelhead has little need to feed after returning from the sea, and that salmon feed not at all. But their survival mechanisms are planted in their genes—and the drive to migrate, spawn, and flee from danger, and the need to eat, are with them from birth. From the time they are alevin struggling out of their egg sacs, to the period of their oceanic journeys, steelhead and salmon must put on the feed bag. When they return from the ocean, steel- head no longer need to eat because their hunger is largely suppressed by hormonal changes taking place as they prepare to spawn. But the instinct doesn't disappear altogether; it only remains dormant. Steelhead can often be seen actively feeding on salmon eggs when salmon are on their redds. And they sometimes eat floating insects. But mostly they are not eating. I believe the old instinct to feed can be triggered momentarily by internal reflexes that occur in response to a particular kind of stimulation. These reflexes don't always come into action, but might be affected by external conditions, such as weather, the depth of the river, the temperature, the time of day, or light conditions. In the end, a steelhead, having no real need to eat, usually spits out what it bites, at least in the case of artificial flies.

I say "bite," but this isn't entirely accurate. Steelhead, like trout and salmon, inhale the water around a fly. The vacuum this creates sucks the fly into the mouth of the fish. For whatever reasons, steelhead will sometimes move to a fly, quite deliberately, with mouth closed, as if to check it out. They might push it out of the water, sink it with a slap of the tail, do everything but balance it on the end of their nose. Some anglers think steelhead "miss" when they strike but don't connect; as if the fish somehow misjudged where the fly would be when it attacked. Or that the steelhead simply changed its mind at the last moment; as if a steelhead even had a mind to change.

When a steelhead appears to be playing with a fly, often the best advice for an angler is to stand fast and refire the cast to the same spot above where the steelhead rose in the first place. You can even try changing flies between casts if you think that will work. Sooner or later the steelhead should get so interested or pissed off, or whatever it is that a steelhead gets, that the fish will inhale the fly and hook himself as he turns to swim back to the bottom.

So that's what I did. I cast back to the same spot where the steelhead had risen, and I watched my fly skitter down the current in a fever of anticipation. This time when the fish rose and I pulled back, I felt the solid weight of a steelhead.

The fish flipped backward into the air and landed with a heavy splash. It tried to bolt downstream. I judged the steelhead to be seven or eight pounds. It jumped again and boiled, thrashing on the surface as my rod tip dipped and danced. I brought the steelhead over into the shallow water and beached it. It was indeed a fish of about eight pounds, a lovely female in silver-and-rose livery. I let the fish slip back into the stream, watching it disappear somewhere on the bottom of the pool.

I had disturbed the pool in my fight with the fish. But I wasn't about to rest the pool, as they say. I was too greedy for another fish. I moved down a few feet and cast again, and I was surprised to see a bulge of water come up around my fly. I cast again, and this time a steelhead took the fly down with a ferocious yank. This was amazing: back-to-back steelhead out of the same pool. Nothing like that had never happened to me before.

The fish pulled and tugged with great vigor. This was an even bigger steelhead than the previous one. Eleven or twelve pounds of steelhead somersaulted out of the water, showering the pool. The steelhead thrashed and boiled on the surface and then sounded. It put up a savage, head-yanking, tail-slapping fight. But it didn't run. If it had, it might have escaped over the pool's shallow tailout and gone down into a rapid below, where I would have been certain to lose it. Instead the fish pulled and tugged and shook itself, trying to rub the leader on the bottom and dislodge itself from whatever it was that was holding him. My rod dipped in long, slow movements for several minutes as the fish struggled on the bottom.

I maneuvered the tiring steelhead over to the beach, where I was able to get a good look at it. The fish would go almost a dozen pounds, of that I was certain. Just as I was leading the fish into the shallows, preparing to beach it, the fly popped out of its mouth and the steelhead went free. Oh, damn! What a performance, though. Two steelhead hooked on dry flies out of the same pool on practically back-to-back casts—that was a personal best. A shame I hadn't been able to land that second fish.

It was midday, so I ate a sandwich for lunch. I believe the Suskwa is also known as the Bear River. I presumed that the word Suskwa meant "bear" in the local Indian tongue. I took out my *Bulkley/Cassiar Forest District Recreation Map (South)*, published by the Forest Service of British Columbia (I like to keep up with all the scholarly journals), and read that section on the back of the map entitled "Safety in Bear and Cougar Country." Lots of free advice: Never store food in tents—keep it in the trunk of your vehicle. Better yet, hang it in a sealed container from a high branch. (Bears have been known to demolish cars and tear off doors to get at the goodies.) Campers were advised to sleep at least fifty meters from the area where they stored and cooked their food. Tents should be pitched away from brush, lakeshores, streambanks, and (my favorite) bear trails. Try and keep clothing and gear free of food odors. Dump dishwater a hundred feet from camp. After meals, burn any tin cans in the campfire. Keep the campsite well policed— don't bury garbage where bears can dig it up. Clean fish in running water. Puncture the bladder and throw the entrails into the running stream or burn them in the campfire. Don't pack or wear herbal-scented perfumes, deodorants, or shampoos. And, ladies, try not to menstruate in the Great Outdoors. Naturally, none of this advice came with any guarantees. In *Green Hills of Africa*, Hemingway wrote: "It is easier to keep well in a good country by taking simple precautions than to pretend that a country which is finished is still good." Amen to that.

The best precaution against bears is probably to stay alert and to make a bit of noise. I like to fish alone, which is not always a wise thing to do in bear habitat. I admit I'm a bit of a coward in the woods. I have been scared by moose and buffalo in Yellowstone National Park. I've even turned chicken at the sight of female elk coming down to drink at the river where I was fishing. But I'd rather put up with a few bears than too many people. One of the reasons I like to fish alone is that in a crowd there is no hiding. Everyone knows if you have blown a hookup, fallen in, or played a fish poorly. Most of all, they know if you cast well or poorly; and in my case it is usually the latter. A bear never criticizes your casting.

I didn't see any bears; and I didn't catch any more steelhead. I fished my way downstream for about a mile. Good country. Once I had gotten away from the parking area beside the bridge, I didn't see any more anglers.

When I returned to the lodge that evening, I found the place pitch-black. Power was out all over the valley. Power failures are quite common up here. The lodge staff was certainly used to this kind of inconvenience. I could hear voices and laughter and the clattering of dinnerware, and smell wonderful aromas coming out of the kitchen and dining room. The staff was managing to cook and serve dinner to everyone by candlelight and battery-powered torchlight. I fished a flashlight out of the boot of my car and gave it to Margaret's sister Betty, to help the girls out. I wolfed down a plate of roast beef, mashed potatoes and gravy, and ate two candy bars for dessert. Then I retired to my room to write in my journal by candlelight. There's something oddly comforting about being in a place where the lights and power go out regularly.

A FISHERMAN FOR LIFE

THE SKEENA, THE "river of mists," drains approximately one-fifth of British Columbia, and is the province's second-largest river. It begins in the mountains of the Stikine Plateau, and for its first two hundred miles it flows in a southerly direction, picking up the Sicintine, Sustut, and Babine Rivers, which come in from the roadless regions to the east. The Skeena continues on a southerly course until it is joined by the Kispiox flowing in from the northwest. Near the town of Hazelton, the Bulkley joins the Skeena from the south. It is here that the Skeena, carrying its own and the combined weight of the other rivers, shifts its course in a southwesterly direction, and the broad, majestic river flows for another two hundred miles until reaching the Pacific near the port town of Prince Rupert. Along the way this stately body of water picks up other salmon and steelhead streams, rivers with fierce Indian glottal-stopping names such as Kitwanga, Zymoetz, Lakelse, Kalum, Exstew, Exchomsiks, Gitnadoix, and Kasiks.

From the moment the river turns westward to flow toward the sea, the great shield of the Skeena Mountains rises to pierce the underclouds. On these mountains warm, moist air from the

Pacific Ocean gets lifted and, when it chills, returns as rainfall or snow to the dark-green forests below. Beyond the Skeenas are even more mountains. The Yellowhead Highway follows the river through a deep, glacier-carved valley. On the morning I drove along the river on my way to Terrace, the blue waters below the glacial mountains appeared to me new and raw, and the river far too broad and deep to fly-fish in any reasonable manner.

Yet fly-fishermen did seek steelhead in the Skeena, searching for them where they rested alongside the shelving bars. There the steelhead could get a break from deep water and the main channel's strong currents. Steelhead bound for the Kispiox, the Babine, the Bulkley, the Sustut, and other famous streams were passing up the main stem of the Skeena. Trophy steelhead were out there, just beyond the thousands of yards of gleaming gravel bars. But I wouldn't have known where to begin looking for one in so much water. When I did catch sight of an angler out there alone on one of the sweeping gravel bars, looking so tiny beside the wide river that flowed under those blue glacier peaks, he appeared to me to be completely dwarfed by his surroundings.

By midday I had reached the logging town of Terrace on the north bank of the Skeena. The land around Terrace once lay under a saltwater fjord. But when the glacier that carved the fjord melted away, the land gradually returned to normal elevation as the seawater retreated back to the coast. I was in the heart of kermodie country. The world's largest concentration of spirit bears was said to be found in the countryside around Terrace. The white bear had become the official symbol of the city. The forests were full of other wildlife, too: moose, bears, and a white mountain goat that was a close relative of the chamois of the Swiss Alps. Terrace was known for its spectacular fishing. A world-record chinook salmon was reeled in from the Skeena River just outside the city limits.

The Skeena Valley also boasted an unusually high concentration of eagles. This was partly due to the presence of the railroad. The Skeena Line of the Grand Trunk Pacific Railway ran through Terrace. The railway connected Prince George in the interior with Prince Rupert on the coast. In Canada they say the railroad built the nation. Canada's network of passenger trains was a lifeline when there were no other forms of transportation into the hinterlands and those lonely expanses of the Canadian prairies. The Prince George–to–Prince Rupert stretch wasn't completed until 1914. The railroad was the principal reason that the Bulkley and Skeena Valleys have such high concentrations of eagles wintering-over in the region. The railway is a meat market. The eagles live on moose and deer killed by the trains. In fact, I am reliably informed that more animals get killed on the railroad tracks than are shot in season by hunters.

I found the cheapest motel in Terrace, the Cedars, and then headed to a nearby tackle shop to purchase a permit to fish the Copper River. I was anxious to see this river, a tributary of the Skeena. It had a reputation as one of the finest steelhead rivers in British Columbia. The folks at the tackle shop told me that the Copper was in the best shape it had been in in weeks. They also warned me to watch out for logging trucks on the narrow dirt road that follows the river, as these trucks gave no quarter.

Naturally I had heard a lot about the destructive logging under way in the Copper River watershed, and I expected to see evidence of clear-cuts and forest devastation. I wasn't prepared for what I actually did see: a mountain valley mantled in shaggy stands of second-growth Sitka spruce. The greenery took my breath away.

It had been forty-five years since the lower watershed had been logged. In slightly more than half a human lifetime, the trees had grown back to full height. Logging operations start at the bottom of a valley and move farther and farther up in time. The mountains of the Copper run all the way up to the toothy crags around Telkwa Pass. A series of logging roads led over the pass from Smithers. Horrible buzzcuts had left the side valleys on both flanks of the Copper unstable. Many of the hills up there had been tonsured, the forest cover completely removed. But all I could see from my vantage point down on the river was green Sitka spruce.

Under a gray sky the Copper looked like greenish soapstone. It once had been a lustrous snowmelt-and-rainwater river, so clear you could see pebbles thirty feet down. But those days were gone. It still looked pretty, though. The Indians called this river the Zymoetz, but white settlers renamed it after the mineral deposits they discovered in the valley.

High up in this narrow mountain valley, well beyond any logging road, and accessible only to hikers and heli-fishermen, the Copper River spilled out of McDonnell Lake, and flowed through alpine meadows into forest highlands. Grizzlies wandered the hillsides and moose browsed on tender shoots of willow and dogwood. The river grew as it was fed by glacial creeks, until it reached full size below the Clore, its major tributary.

The Clore is a big problem for fly-fishermen. It hosts a run of native steelhead, and the fishing on the Clore can be quite good. But when it rains, the Clore and everything below it, including the Copper River all the way down to the Skeena, can turn into a grayish mess that takes days to clear. The problem is the Clore Slide. A bank made up of unstable marine clays—what local river guides call "blue moon shit"—slopes downward into the Clore River at a 45-degree angle. The trees above are thirty feet away from the slope, so there is little to stabilize the bank. The logging companies say the Clore Slide is a natural phenomenon and not their fault, as there is no logging in the forest directly above the sliding bank. This is only a half-truth, and thus a lie by omission. The logging companies are very much at fault. Miles of buzzcuts along the upper Clore have destabilized the watershed, changing the whole hydrology of the narrow valley. With so much of the forest cover missing, and the ground rendered so unstable, soil that has become saturated with heavy rain or snowfall can't be held back. When it rains, a violent discharge comes gushing out of the Clore. The out-of-control river rises and eats away at the foot of the clay bank, ruining everything downstream of the Clore Slide, and discoloring the lower Copper River all the way out to where it empties into the Skeena.

This was one of the most beautiful river valleys I had ever seen. From the logging road on which I was driving, I could see mile after mile of classic steelhead drifts lying out there between generous gravel bars. At one point the logging road seemed to rise steeply, but it was really the river dropping into a deep chasm, the first of two canyons accessible only to the most intrepid fishermen. Down in the canyons one could find debris logs perched as high as fifty feet above the river, a testament to storms and the Copper's seasonal ferocity. Because of their steep gradients, the Copper and its tributaries didn't take well to clear-cutting up in the hills. Devastating floods occur with ever-increasing frequency, ripping out trees, stripping away banks, and cutting out new channels.

The logging road came out level with the river once again. I had been advised that the farther upstream I drove, the better the pools would be, the cleaner the river, and the greater my chance of hooking a Copper River steelhead. At a sign marked Kilometer 33, I came upon the mouth of the Clore River. A fly-fisherman was casting in the pool that formed at the junction of the two rivers. Upstream, the Copper was running slightly clearer than it was below the Clore, without so much of that chalky-green water. The Clore had been named after a West Virginia prospector, Arthur Clore, a black man who had called Canada "the land of hope."

The logging road passed high above a second canyon, came out level with the river once again, and ended abruptly at a place called the Fossil Beds. I turned around and drove back downriver, all the way to a sign marked Kilometer 15. I found a narrow turnout on the logging road that allowed me to park without maybe getting clipped by a logging truck. A path led through the alders down to a wide gravel bar several thousand yards long. I was looking at one of the most beautiful steelhead pools I had ever beheld. From its head downstream to the tail-out lay about eight hundred yards of ideal steelhead drift. Rising above the river were mountains of dense Sitka spruce. Only one hilltop in the distance showed a bald head, a single tonsure, evidence of the logging that was eating away at the pristine environment.

I crossed the wide gravel bar, making my way among uneven cobblestones bleached pale by the sun. When I got to the head of the pool, I waded knee-deep into the water and tied a dry fly on to the end of my leader. The gliding water appeared smooth and polished, reflecting the sky and the evergreens. Really, I couldn't have designed a more lovely steelhead run.

My first cast was so short as to seem to have little real fishing in it. But steelhead often lie close to a bank, much closer than we think. Steelhead fishermen have a tendency to begin with very long casts, sometimes overlooking prime water. I wasn't going to make the mistake of wading or casting beyond the range of the resting fish. With each new cast, I lengthened my line by a few feet, until I reached a maximum length that I felt comfortable with. From then on it was just a matter of taking a few steps downstream after each cast. Because I made it a point not to wade out too far, all my casts would finish close by the bank, no matter how far out I cast.

I could sense the steelhead waiting in the skinny water, camouflaged against the river's sunlit, pebbly bottom. My dry fly cut a low V across the lustrous surface. I was told that Copper River steelhead find dry flies irresistible. They are known to snap at natural mayflies that float on the current, even this late in autumn.

I passed down the entire length of the run, but I got no rises with my dry fly. So I returned to the head of the pool, and this time I tied on a wet-fly pattern known as a Green Butt Skunk, a rather ubiquitous pattern here in the Pacific Northwest. They say it was invented by a fellow named Dan Callaghan, an Oregon steelhead fisherman rather renowned for his photographs of the North Umpqua River. I probably have a dozen or so of these patterns in my fly box. I fished this fly using a so-called "greased line" method, that is, with a floating line and a few gentle mends to slow the swing, with the fly floating just an inch or two under the surface with very little drag.

On a river like the Copper, I couldn't see any point in fishing any other way than on or near the surface. The simplest way to bring a summer steelhead to a fly—on top—is also the most exciting. A steelhead rising to a fly is always a heart-stopping sight. For some reason the fight seems more animated when the fish is taken on top rather than on the bottom. At least that's been my experience. And let's face it, it's also easier fishing with a floating line than dredging a heavy sinker along the bottom. And I'm always one to take the easy way out.

For a long time there was nothing. And then I thought I saw a shape rise beneath my fly, tracking it underwater. On my next cast, a solid shape rose out of the liquid refraction and pushed a transparent membrane, all that separated the worlds of water and air. The water bulged, and in my excitement I struck before actually feeling the weight of the fish—a cardinal error committed. Trout fishermen are trained to set the hook almost immediately when they see a trout rise to their fly. But steelhead fisherman are enjoined from striking, raising the rod, or taking any action whatsoever until they actually feel the weight of the fish. It's hard to steady the nerves and discipline yourself this way in the excitement of a rise.

On my next cast, a steelhead rose out of the many moving reflections down there on the stream bottom and sucked the fly down hard. I felt the weight, and when I struck, the fish jumped, popping the hook, freeing itself immediately. One tantalizing, electric jolt, and then nothing. From the briefest glimpse I had of that leaping steelhead, I figured I'd just lost a seven-pound fish.

I touched up the point of the hook with a file I keep in a vest pocket for just such a purpose, and sent the fly on its way again. I made many more casts, moving slowly down the pool. And then suddenly—wham!—another strike. A heavy steelhead turned and swam away with my fly. I pulled up on the rod and the steelhead erupted out of the river, landed with a splat, and tore about on the surface, shaking itself, spray flying everywhere. My rod plunged down one last time with exceptional violence and sprang back quite lifeless. Another fish off, another clean escape. No doubt about it, though, this steelhead was larger than the first one. At least I had gotten a good, satisfying look when it jumped.

The late-afternoon sun slipped behind the forested mountains and now there was a noticeable chill in the air. But I didn't want to leave the pool with this kind of action going on. I fished the entire length of the pool a third time, but I had no more strikes. In the coldness that accompanied dusk, the evergreen forest darkened, but I continued fishing long after most of the light had drained away from the valley.

I made the short drive back to Terrace along the dark Skeena River, bought a couple of fast-food hamburgers in town, and took them back to my motel room. I turned on the television; except for a few rubbishy Canadian programs, most of the shows on both the network and cable bands had originated in the United States. Even the hamburgers came from an American-owned fast-food chain. Canadians see a profound difference in our cultures, but we Americans are apt to notice very little change at all. Even when we are visiting, we are barely aware that we have left home. We are jolted back to the realization that we are in a foreign land only after someone like a store clerk hands us our change back in Canadian currency, and we have to count carefully those confusing dollar-coin denominations.

I awoke early the next morning to a pounding rain. I drove out on Kalum Lake Drive to visit Noel Gyger, chairman of the Terrace District Angling Guides Association. He operates a lodge called Northwest Fishing Guides just outside of town. Noel takes anglers out on guided fishing trips on the Skeena, Copper, Kitimat, and other nearby salmon and steelhead rivers. Earlier Noel had invited me on a float with one of his guides, but a last-minute booking from paying clients had forced Noel to cancel the trip. I had been looking forward to getting out on a river like the Skeena. Still, I'd have a chance to talk with Noel.

"I just got a group of British anglers off on the river," Noel said, greeting me at the door of his house in the pouring rain. "I call them 'old shakeys.' They're rather elderly gentlemen, and they're all members of the same fly-fishing club. You should have seen them out there, all wrapped up in rainwear and mufflers, in the best British tradition."

Terrace also gets a large contingent of visiting anglers from "the Continent." The Skeena is advertised heavily in overseas fishing magazines. There are lodges around Terrace that are owned and operated by German immigrants who cater specifically to European fly-fishermen. They rent jetboats and driftboats to their clients and advise them where to fish. This rubs Noel the wrong way, as he feels that these lodge owners, who are not licensed guides like he is, are in effect "guiding." The amount a guide pays for his license is determined by the number of "rod days" granted him to take out clients on various rivers. Noel pays upward of $6,500 annually for his license.

"These B&Bs are popping up all over and taking away business from the licensed lodges," he said. We sipped cups of steaming tea at his kitchen table. Everything about his house screamed fishing. There were fishing mounts all over the walls, and framed photographs of clients proudly displaying their catches. Fishing magazines lined shelves or rested in neat stacks on several coffee tables. In his living room, I noticed a plaque hanging on the wall that read:

I am a fisherman for life.

It's not something I do.
It's who I am.

Fishing is not an escape.

It is where I belong,
where I am supposed to be.

It is not a place.
but a life-long journey.

"These B&Bs are really fishing lodges," Noel told me, warming to his subject, "although they operate as bed-and-breakfasts. The guests belong to private fishing clubs back in Europe, where there's hardly any fishing left at all. They've seized the opportunity to have set up shop in Terrace. They advertise in magazines—'Come on out to Terrace.' They won't guide—that would be illegal without a license—but they'll rent you a boat and rods, tell you where to fish, and send you out on your own. A B&B owner will say: 'Here, just rent my car and go on up to the Copper.' Now, that's a bit cheaper than what a lodge like ours has to charge. Technically speaking, what they're doing isn't illegal, but it's got to change."

The Copper is the most popular steelhead river around Terrace, and the angling pressure is great. "The pools are becoming overcrowded," Noel said. "It's causing big problems, and the angling guides aren't the cause of these problems."

Noel, who employs two guides at his lodge, buys only thirty-three licensed rod days a year on the Copper. "It's a great fly-fishing river in the fall, a great steelhead river," he said. "With thirty-three rod days, I'm not going to overpressure it. In the fall, I take sports out to the Copper one or two times. Then I'll take them over to the Kitimat, to the Kasiks, and the Kalum, and maybe on up to the Meziadin. We move them around, so we don't put pressure on any one place. There's only so much room on some of these rivers, only so many pools. They're becoming too popular. We have to decide whether to manage the sport or let it go to the wind and let free enterprise take over and let her rip."

An angler has a great deal to choose from in this part of the Skeena region. Salmon and steelhead are entering the Skeena from the ocean every day of the year. The fishing year begins in January with a run of winter steelies. A separate race of spring steelhead can be found coming into the rivers from March through early June. From May through mid-August, king salmon come into the Skeena and swim up into the larger tributary rivers. The world's record chinook on rod and reel, 92½ pounds, was caught in the Skeena less than five minutes outside Terrace. Starting in July, and continuing on through September, sockeye and pink salmon will be making their spawning runs. From mid-August, and lasting through mid-October, coho salmon come pouring into the streams. And in what is perhaps the prime fishing opportunity of the year, summer-run steelhead start showing up in the rivers around early August, with the peak fishing lasting through the end of autumn. A so-called "fall run" of steelhead, a separate race of fish from the "summer run," follows in late November, rounding out the fishing year.

"In the spring, I like to take my sports out on the Kalum," Noel said. "The Kalum gets four runs of steelhead: winter, spring, summer, and fall. They're all separate races of fish, but they winter over and spawn at the same time in the spring, right around the middle of May. Now, what I'll do, I'll only target them from March 15 until April 15. We could be guiding for them ten months out of the year; but we don't want to be pulling on them that long. So for conservation reasons, I've restricted my license on the Kalum to rod days from mid-March to mid-October. In the fall, we hardly fish it very much at all, as the steelhead really aren't in the Kalum in any great numbers and the water is too high. Most of the fall run doesn't get in until the end of October and November; and we don't guide at that time. This is a restriction we wanted—it's what the angling guides want. We fish for very short periods. I like the spring. The Kalum is a very special, very unique river in the springtime."

Noel told me about the experience of one of his fly-fishing clients, Robert Tomes of Chicago, who managed to land a wild Kalum steelhead that measured forty-one inches in length and twenty-five inches around the girth. Tomes released the fish, possibly a world record on the fly rod.

"It was a big buck steelhead," Noel said. "Now, according to the catch-and-release formula [a system of measuring length and girth to calculate a fish's weight with reliable accuracy], that fish could have weighed thirty-four pounds." Had Tomes kept that fish, it might have beaten Karl Mausser's fly-rod record set more than thirty years ago on the Kispiox River.

"Tomes and a guide were fishing in a pool where the water was fairly fast," Noel told me. "He paid exact attention to what the guide told him. He rigged up with a T-300 [a heavy sinking line with 300 grains of weight, the very line I had been using and cursing when I was on the Kispiox] and a 15-pound Max-

ima leader [a brand of monofilament line known for its resistance to abrasion], and that's what saved the day. He had to
put a lot of torque on that fish to get him to turn."

One very special river for Noel is the Kasiks. In the fall, Noel
takes his clients on the Kasiks to fish for coho salmon. The
Kasiks is a true wilderness river, and Noel compares it to the
more famous Babine. Noel made a point of telling me that his
clients are known to refer to the Kasiks as "the most beautiful
river in the world."

"It's the one river in our area that's still virgin, hasn't been
touched," said Noel. "There's no road up there. There's only
a natural-gas pipeline, and it doesn't always follow the river. In
order to do maintenance on it, they have to get in by helicopter.
The canyon is very narrow with a very steep gradient. So it's
not feasible for loggers to go in and log it out, as they've done
in a number of our other valleys. The Kasiks is much too narrow for logging."

Noel takes his clients into the Kasiks by jetboat, running up
from the Skeena. The Kasiks is strictly a salmon river; there are
no steelhead whatsoever in it.

"Being a small river, the steelhead don't winter over," Noel
explained. "And it really doesn't have the right kind of gravel
that steelhead like to spawn in. Steelhead this far north like a
rugged, boulder river, and the Kasiks has more of a sandy bottom. The salmon can get by with that. The Kasiks is closed to
fishing for chinook, so we only target cohos."

Another little-known river that Noel likes to take his clients
on is the Meziadin, a very short river, only about three miles in

length, that flows out of a lake. "We call it our insurance river," Noel said. "And I kind of compare it to Babine Lake. The river comes out of the lake and remains relatively clear. When you have three miles of river coming out of a lake, you won't be getting glacial melt. It has great steelheading in the fall, and great rainbow-trout-fishing. The rainbows come out of the lake to spawn in the springtime; so to protect them, the river's closed to angling until June 15."

Noel pointed to a framed photograph that he had blown up to the size of a poster, one of many such photographs adorning the walls of Noel's home showing clients cradling trophy fish. "That's the lodge record for a coho salmon, a twenty-seven-pounder," Noel said. "It was caught on the Kasiks." He pointed to another photograph showing an angler displaying a king salmon of almost incomprehensible girth. "That's the lodge record for a chinook, eighty-three pounds," said Noel. "We caught that on the Kalum River." Noel directed my attention to a third framed photograph: the lodge record for a steelhead, a thirty-two-pound buck, also out of the Kalum.

The walls of Noel's house were decorated with many more photographs and trophy mounts of steelhead and salmon. And every shelf seemed lined with orderly stacks of magazines and videocassettes all given over to the sport. I flipped through some of the magazines; some covers boasted fish reeled in by Noel's clients. Noel's own Internet postings reporting on the fishing around Terrace had all been carefully catalogued. I asked Noel about the plaque with the fisherman's credo on that begins, "I am a fisherman for life . . ."

"I have no idea who wrote that," Noel said. "I got it off

another fishing guide. It caught my eye and I copied it down. I see fishing as my calling."

Noel told me that he was raised by his grandfather, who took him fishing all the time. His grandfather particularly enjoyed fly-fishing for rainbow trout in lakes. He said his grandfather was the major influence in his life.

"My grandfather was fifty-four years old when he retired from the railroad and started his own business," Noel said. "I'm fifty-three now, and I think of how my grandpa wanted to start a business at fifty-four. It was the Evergreen Funeral Home, in Smithers. What that did was inspire me to want to own my own business, too. It really didn't matter to me what that business was, so long as it was my own. When my grandpa passed away, I inherited the funeral home."

"So you were once a mortician," I said.

"Yeah. And later I was in the logging business, and the trucking business, and the catering business. And what I found out was that after five years or so I'd get tired, or things wouldn't work out, or I wasn't making enough money—and with the logging business I went broke. And what hit me, what I always came back to in my life, was fishing.

"I had been living as a businessman for twenty-five years, but I wasn't always successful. So I went and I got a real job, I became a bread salesman. And I built up a route in Terrace, and it really went well; and it was almost like my own business. But the company was always after me to do more and sell more. The only thing that saved me was that I could go fishing on my days off." Noel paused to refill our teacups with steaming water.

"When you work for somebody," he said, "you'll maybe get just this two-week vacation or holiday every year. So for this one vacation in 1983, my friend and I went fishing on the Kalum River, and we caught that eighty-three-pound chinook that you see in the photograph. All of a sudden, this business mind of mine starts clicking. Here we've caught an eighty-three-pound chinook, probably the biggest ever taken out of the river. Hey, maybe we can start a business.

"So we started a publication, *Big Fish Country*, maybe in 1984 or '85. We wrote articles and stories to cover Terrace and Prince Rupert and Smithers. And in addition to publishing *Big Fish Country*, we sold souvenirs, like hats and T-shirts. And eventually we got involved in guiding. In those days, it was only fifty bucks for a license.

"Now, back to this business thing again. I'm fifty-three, and when I turn fifty-four, I know I'm going to be thinking about my grandpa. And I'll think that this is what I should have been doing in the first place. But young people, sometimes they get trapped in situations, or in an occupation or a job or whatever. But you know, you really need to have a job that you love. And for me that's fishing. I now realize it's what I should have been doing all along.

"I've been obsessive with all my businesses. But after five years of it, I'd get tired or go broke. But fishing has never been that way for me. Fishing to me isn't even about making money. It's something that's always been on my mind even when I was a little kid. And after fifteen years of it as a business, I'm not sick of it, and I love it more and more.

"It's now coming up on the year 2000, and I love this business all the more, and I never want to get out. Now, someday I may no longer be the lodge owner; and I may get too old to handle the rod days. And somebody else will be running the lodge. But I'm always going to be involved in fishing in some way. I've found my calling."

It was still raining hard when I left Noel, so I decided that instead of fishing I would drive all the way out to the end of the Yellowhead Highway and see the port city of Prince Rupert, where the Skeena broadens out into the Pacific. The great river grew ever wider as I drove toward the coast. The gravel banks along the Skeena gleamed in the rain, and the mist swirled up into the dank green mountains. The trees were giants, reaching a hundred feet and more above the ground. Western hemlocks mostly, their droopy tops and feathery branches rising up amid huge cedars, Douglas firs thirty feet in girth, and a lush floor of giant rain-forest ferns. The shaggy greenery seemed to grow wherever it could take root in the ground.

The ice-capped Coast Mountains had been cut by a rich Pacific estuary at the mouth of the Skeena. The sea channels and islands around Prince Rupert once were the site of dozens of Tsimshian villages. The tribes wintered at the mouth of the estuary, and in summer followed the salmon up the Skeena in their cedar-bark canoes. Today Prince Rupert is a maritime crossing for ferry passengers going north to Alaska, across the strait to the Queen Charlotte Islands, or Vancouver Island to the south. The famous Inside Passage to Canada and Alaska followed fjords that cut their way into the mountainous coast. Alaska was only fifty miles away. Directly across the water from

Prince Rupert lay the huge offshore archipelagoes known as the Queen Charlottes. These green islands were actually the tops of mountains rising out of the Pacific Ocean. Each island was covered in evergreens, and the hills were laced with salmon streams. The Queen Charlottes were the nesting grounds for half of British Columbia's sea lions and a quarter of its seabirds. More than twenty thousand gray whales passed by each year on a journey north to the Bering Sea. The world's greatest population of killer whales swam in these waters. And the world's largest concentration of grizzly bears was found back on the mainland in the nearby Kutzeymateen Valley.

I found myself in a landscape of gray, moist Pacific light. With so much rain, cloud cover, and swirling vapor, I was beginning to think it doubtful that I would ever have a chance on this trip to see the Northern Lights, those luminous bands that sometimes appear in the night sky at this northerly latitude. Also known as the northern aurora, or aurora borealis, the bands of light are believed to come from high-energy protons streaming over into the atmosphere, electrical discharges in the ionized air that slip through the earth's magnetic shield, an event that sometimes occurs when the sun is in a particularly active state.

John Fennelly had been privileged to see the Northern Lights on one of his visits. He had been camping at Johanson Lake, and had awakened in the shank of night to wolves barking. There was no wind, and he could see every star in the sky.

Shooting skyward from beyond the range were six separate beams of Northern Lights. They spread out in the shape of a fan, and brought to mind the rays of the rising sun on the Japanese flag. These shafts of light were white and unwavering. Two of them were so brilliant that it was hard to believe they were not produced by huge military searchlights directly behind the crest of the range.

Not a breath of air stirred. From all points of the compass came the baying of timber wolves. I say "baying" because the sound was very different from the mournful song those wolves give forth in the dead of winter. It was a prolonged deep bark, repeated endlessly in regular slow cadence.

I wouldn't be seeing the aurora borealis tonight, of that I was certain. The rain had let up, but the low overcast was like a freshly spawned milt. Everything from the clam-gray sky to the dripping forest seemed connected to its own watery reflection.

The dark rain forest seemed to manufacture its own particular brand of gloom. I could imagine the tribes living frightened by the edges of such deep forests. In his book *Passage to Juneau*, Jonathan Raban writes that the dark that loomed within the forests of the Pacific Northwest must have filled the Indians with a terror of the unknown. The stories they told around their campfires were peopled with killer whales and bears that were always leaping out of nature's Peaceful Kingdom to kill them. For these Indian animists, who made little distinction between what could be seen and what was merely hidden in an invisible world behind this one, the monsters of their imagination lived on an equal footing with the animals of the forest and the sea, and a grizzly bear standing on its hind legs could easily be a Sasquatch.

Curiously, this far north, I noticed very little Bigfoot tourist hokum. The farther you got from civilization, the less you heard about Bigfoot. Or at least that Bigfoot who appeared in the tabloids, as opposed to the shadowy figment of Indian animism. Bigfoot was big in the more urbanized areas. Up here in the wilderness he hardly seemed to matter at all. As I was coming up here, driving along the Fraser River, in the southerly and more populated portion of the province, I had passed by Harrison Hot Springs, where there had been dozens of purported Sasquatch sightings in the surrounding mountains. But the farther I penetrated into the backcountry, the less interest there seemed to be in this phantom, at least as a tourist phenomenon.

I expect that Bigfoot, or at least the Sasquatch that has been adopted by white people as part of our modern geek show, fills some kind of psychological need for those of us who no longer have any real wilderness left. Naturally Bigfoot is huge in northern California.

Superstition insults the majesty of the real. People who can't imagine the world around them as it truly exists have lost the capacity for true wonder. But to the Indians, Bigfoot was not superstition but rather an extension of their everyday lives. The Sasquatch of Indian animism did resemble the world they lived in, a rather frightening and mysterious realm filled with real monsters that leapt out to bring sudden death. Our modern reincarnation of Sasquatch in all its goonery resembles nothing so much as our tabloid and consumer culture. The desire by modern man to believe in Sasquatches, as with alien visitations and flights of angels, might relate to a hunger for transcendence or a need to escape the ordinariness of daily life. But there is nothing ordinary about the Pacific Northwest, at least that portion of it that remains a true wilderness. The reality of that wilderness seems enough to challenge the human imagination forever. It's Bigfoot that has become banal.

A RUN OF SALMON

THE COPPER RIVER was blown out from the rain of the previous day. So I thought I would drive out to the Lakelse River for some salmon fishing. I had considered sampling the steelhead fishing on the Kitimat River. But the Kitimat, which lies south in a drainage separate from the Skeena system, is prone to clouding from rain and glacial runoff. The Kitimat empties into the Douglas Channel, and is a major spawning ground for eulachon, a small, oily fish also known as candlefish, once used as both food and fuel by the Indians. Coastal and interior Indians established elaborate eulachon trade routes known as "grease trails," said to be the most elaborate network of Indian trails in North America.

I was fully aware that eighty percent of the forest cover around the Lakelse River had been removed by logging. But I was told the river would run relatively clear after a rain because its gradient wasn't as steep and unforgiving as the Copper's. Logging wouldn't have affected the clarity of the water quite as much. Bruce Hill, a campaigner for the Sierra Club and a past president of the Steelhead Society of British Columbia, told me that the Lakelse might be the world's most productive salmon river, if you took into account the biomass of salmon and compared it against the stream's relatively short length. Hill said that the Lakelse was better than anything one could find in Alaska, at least in terms of the sheer density of the coho coming into it. Only eleven kilometers long, the Lakelse hosted runs of pink salmon that in some years topped a million fish. The pinks were followed by a run of cohos, sometimes as many as forty thousand fish. Imagine, forty thousand coho salmon in only three miles of river.

Steelhead and salmon are essentially the same fish. To be sure, there are differences among the Pacific salmon, the Atlantic salmon, the steelhead, and the various sea trouts. But they are minor. All these fish are more alike than they are dissimilar. There are, however, enough differences to make it matter to fly-fishermen when it comes to the techniques necessary to catch them on a fly rod. Leave it to fly-fishermen to make life even more complicated than it already is.

Steelhead and all Pacific salmon are classified under the same genus, *Oncorhynchus*. Officially they are classified as a subspecies of one another. But in behavior, steelhead seem more closely related to *Salmo salar*, the Atlantic salmon, than they are to their Pacific cousins. Millions of years ago, the Atlantic and Pacific were joined together as one ocean. When the land and ice that is North America rose up, the oceans separated, and Atlantic and Pacific salmon, or at least their forebears, continued down separate evolutionary paths. An Atlantic salmon is more like a steelhead than a Pacific salmon, and not only from the fly-fisherman's perspective. Pacific salmon spawn only once and then die—there is no exception to this rule. But Atlantic salmon and steelhead might spawn two or even three times before completing their life journey. The percentage that does survive the first spawning run is somewhat small. I don't know the exact ratio for steelhead survival; but nine out of every ten Atlantic salmon die after making their first spawning run (and of the surviving ten percent, nine out of ten will be females).

Fly-fishermen consider Atlantic salmon and steelhead fishing to be essentially the same kind of sport. Unlike Pacific salmon, steelhead and Atlantic salmon lose little of their fighting strength as they swim upriver toward their spawning grounds. They are powerful fish, but like all salmonids, they can't swim hard for long distances without needing a rest. Because their bodies can't get a sufficient amount of oxygen during a violent exertion, they can be landed in a reasonable amount of time. This is probably the only reason fly-fishermen are even able to land them on their slender wands. Ultimately these great fish are unable to resist the pull of an angler's line. It's imperative to play and land a salmon or a steelhead as quickly as possible if you intend to release these fish back into the river. Salmon and steelhead need to be revived before succumbing to a fatal buildup of lactic acid—the same thing that causes your muscles to burn during a strenuous workout.

Atlantic salmon and steelhead fishermen are forever arguing about which fish is strongest. Lee Wulff, a salmon fisherman extraordinaire, has pointed out that the fastest fish swimming in the ocean are those with stiff tails, such as members of the mackerel family, which includes bluefin tuna, the fastest fish in the ocean. (Bluefin have been clocked at sixty miles per hour, just five miles per hour short of the land speed record set by the world's fastest mammal, the cheetah.) A salmon's tail is slightly stiffer than a steelhead's. For this reason, you can tail an Atlantic salmon by hand easier than you can a steelhead. Wulff believed this stiffer tail gives Atlantic salmon a slight edge over steelhead in the strength department. Also, Atlantic salmon simply grow larger than steelhead, and there's no denying the appeal of size when it comes to sport fishing. Steelhead won't grow much over twenty-five pounds; a thirty-pounder is a real event. On the other hand, fly-fishermen have caught a few Atlantic salmon in the fifty- and sixty-pound class. But those were rare fish. Most fly-fishermen will find themselves tussling with steelhead and Atlantic salmon of about equal weight and size.

Anyway, the issue of size and strength can be a relative matter. A fifteen-pound steelhead caught in a river very near the ocean, and only a few days out of the saltwater, will put up a better fight than an Atlantic salmon of the same weight that has been caught far upriver, and vice versa.

Although Atlantic salmon and steelhead are more alike in behavior than they are dissimilar, again there are enough differences to make it matter from the point of view of a fly-fisherman. One major difference between the two species is that while all salmon stop feeding the moment they enter fresh water, steelhead may continue to feed sporadically, albeit very little. The hormonal change that triggers the spawning run basically shuts down their appetites. The stomach shrinks to accommodate the production of eggs and milt. Neither fish needs the nutrition at this point; each can survive for months in a river on the energy reserves they have accumulated from their time in the ocean.

I have never fished for Atlantic salmon. That is a dereliction of duty and I hope someday to make up for it. So whatever I have learned about the technical differences between steelhead and Atlantic salmon fishing comes to me secondhand.

Both Atlantic salmon and summer steelhead will rise readily to the surface and move a considerable distance to attack a fly. But an Atlantic salmon will be inclined to move somewhat farther. Atlantic salmon seem to like a fly that's moving a little faster than the current; steelhead don't. For this reason, steelhead anglers often mend their line, a maneuver that slows down the speed of the fly. Atlantic salmon anglers rarely mend, unless it is to speed up the fly. All fly anglers are advised that when they see a salmon or a steelhead hit the fly, they should wait until they actually feel the full weight of the fish before setting the hook. Many fly-fishermen, overcome by the visual excitement of a rise, strike too soon; and they either snatch the fly away from the fish, or even pull it right out of its mouth, literally snatching defeat from the jaws of victory.

An Atlantic salmon might seize a fly in a somewhat slower and more deliberate manner than a steelhead. And they don't seem to panic so much when hooked; instead Atlantic salmon take off in a steady run sometimes highlighted by a few graceful leaps. But steelhead are known to explode the moment they feel the prick of a hook. Jumping five or six times in the first few seconds, they cartwheel and turn somersaults, and make line-smoking runs. In short, they simply go berserk.

Both Atlantic salmon and steelhead tend to hold in rivers in spots where the current is to their liking. They seem more willing to strike freely and take lures immediately upon entering a freshwater river than they will later on, after they have become somewhat more acclimated to the changes from salt to fresh water. Like all salmonids and trout, they face into the current at all times (just as they did as smolts, always facing upstream and riding the current backwards to the sea). They adjust their holding positions with the rise and fall of the river. They prefer a current that is moving at the same speed as a man can comfortably walk. Atlantic salmon prefer to remain in relatively open water, perhaps as a throwback to their time in the ocean. Steelhead react more like the trout they are, seeking the protection of ledges, midstream boulders, undercut banks, and overhanging tree limbs. Both salmon and steelhead attack a lure more readily when they are in relatively shallow water. The fish are much harder to catch when they are holed up in deep pools with a slow current.

Salmon and steelhead entering a river early, spawn around the same time as fish that arrive late. Salmon spawn in autumn; steelhead in early spring. Atlantic salmon might begin returning from the sea in the late springtime or early summer. New fish will keep coming into the river right through October. Steelhead can be found entering a river any month of the year, depending on the type of runs hosted by a particular river. For example, some rivers host runs of spring, summer, fall, and winter steelhead. For the fly-fisherman, this means you can fish for steelhead all year, but only half the year for Atlantic salmon.

There is one more major difference between Atlantic salmon and steelhead fishing that really needs to be pointed out here.

And it is the most crucial difference of all. Steelhead fishing is relatively affordable; Atlantic salmon fishing is prohibitively expensive. At least it is for me.

If an Atlantic salmon trip is beyond my financial means, there is little to stop me from fishing for Pacific salmon. And yet oddly enough, fly-fishing for Pacific salmon on the West Coast is not nearly as popular as fly-fishing for steelhead. This has something to do with the way Pacific salmon behave after they enter freshwater streams. For starters, they lose their oceanic brightness and vigor rather quickly.

On the West Coast, the first salmon to arrive are kings. The kings come in two runs, one in spring and another in fall. The spring salmon are usually heading into larger and more distant rivers. They will summer-over in those rivers before spawning in autumn. They are good sport on a fly rod for about a month after they enter the river; then they begin to deteriorate and lose their power. Fall-run salmon are more abundant and darken even more quickly after coming into fresh water. There is only a limited window of opportunity for the fly-fisherman, who must pursue his sport while the salmon are still fresh.

King salmon, as the name implies, are the largest of the five species of Pacific salmon. They can weigh more than fifty pounds and will strain even the stoutest tackle. Kings are also called chinook salmon, after a Salish Indian tribe, and a warm wind peculiar to the Pacific Northwest. A shimmering silver in the ocean, king salmon change color, reddening rather quickly in the case of autumn fish, as they enter freshwater to spawn. They can be magnificent sport on rod and line either while in the ocean or just a few days after entering a river. But the farther they travel upriver, and the more time they spend away from the sea, the less fight and determination king salmon will have. Spawning males blacken and spawning females turn a brass color before dying.

King salmon are becoming increasingly popular to pursue with a fly rod. But that wasn't always the case. For a long time it was believed by Pacific Northwest fishermen that king salmon couldn't be taken on a fly rod at all. Fly-fishermen found the king salmon almost impossible to tempt up from the bottom with a fly that was fished near the surface. They couldn't to be taken with the "greased lining" methods so popular with Atlantic salmon and steelhead fishermen.

In time fly-fishermen discovered that if they used heavy sinking lines to reach the fish where they rested near the bottom, these salmon could be caught. Handling such big ordnance and heavy rods wasn't to everyone's liking at first. But the sport has slowly grown in popularity, and king salmon draw large numbers of fly-fishermen to places like Alaska, where kings are particularly abundant and more easily caught. When still fresh, king salmon will take flies readily, but only if they are fished rather deep, in the same column of water that the salmon are swimming in. They won't chase a fly far, the way an Atlantic salmon or a steelhead will. King salmon aren't show-offs—they don't like to waste energy. When a king strikes, he does so with a kind of magisterial authority, and there's no mistaking the yank. A king salmon is capable of taking a lot of line on a run, and makes graceful leaps and jumps. The tug-of-war can last for an hour or more, especially if an angler is geared up for smaller fish like steelhead. In the old days, steelhead fly-fishermen who accidentally hooked king salmon made a habit of breaking the fish off deliberately rather than spend hours fighting it. In those cases, the kings had likely been in the river for a long time and lost much of their liveliness and appeal.

In terms of sheer numbers, sockeyes, chums, and pink salmon reign in the Pacific Northwest. Sadly, these fish are no longer important in my home state, California. But they run in incredible numbers up in Alaska and British Columbia. Sock-eyes are also known as red salmon. In salt water these sockeyes appear metallic, with speckled, greenish blue backs. But when they enter freshwater rivers to spawn, their trunks turn fire-engine–red, and their heads and tails turn bright green. The sight of thousands of red salmon pouring into shallow rivers in Alaska is one of the most glorious sights in nature. The sockeyes are not big, averaging only five to seven pounds, and they are not really a fly-rod fish per se. Most fly anglers accidentally catch them by inadvertently snagging them. In fact, a hook embedded anywhere near a sockeye's mouth is considered a "fair take" in most angling circles. But sockeye have actually been known to move a few feet to deliberately attack a fly. And a tiny number of anglers who can work relatively small flies through shallow riffles when the sockeye are on the move are known to enjoy success from time to time. Although the sock-eye is not highly rated as a fly-rod fish, it makes screaming runs that can take an angler well into his fly line and backing.

Another salmon not particularly popular with fly rodders, despite their prolific numbers, is the chum or dog salmon. But fly-fishermen can enjoy scores of hookups in a single day when chums are in the river. The chums are the second-largest of the

Pacific salmon, averaging between eight and eighteen pounds in weight. Fresh chums are known to take a fly with a very violent hit. Within hours or even a few days of entering a river, chums can be taken on top with surface flies, a very unusual feat for a Pacific salmon. Later fly-fishermen will have to go deeper for them with sinking lines. In their ocean phase, chums, like all the Pacific salmon, have midnight-blue backs and silver sides. But upon entering the estuaries, they develop red-and-purple longitudinal splotches. The spawning males grow caninelike teeth, which accounts for their other name, dog salmon. They are extremely powerful fish, jumping and taking out line when hooked.

Pink salmon are the most abundant. They don't run into all rivers every year; rather, peak runs occur in odd-or even-numbered years, depending on the particular river systems. This wasn't a "pink year" in northern British Columbia—and yet I saw pink salmon everywhere. Pinks are not great jumpers; but when hooked they are vigorous head shakers, and make short, surging runs. They also darken quickly after entering fresh water and soon lose their vitality.

For the sport fisherman, the coho or silver salmon is considered the gamest on a fly rod. It is the one Pacific salmon that comes closest to acting like a steelhead. Silver salmon fresh from the ocean will even take dry flies, incredible as that seems. They will move farther for a fly, and rise more readily, than any other Pacific salmon. They are also fairly large, averaging six to twelve pounds, with a few tipping the scales around thirty pounds. In short, they are the same size as steelhead, and can be taken on the same tackle. While in the ocean, cohos are like freshly stamped silver; once in the rivers they remain brighter and stay in prime fighting condition a lot longer than the other Pacific salmon. They are aerial acrobats when hooked and can make line-burning sprints. In general, coho salmon angling represents light tackle fishing at its best. The liveliness of silver salmon, their willingness to chase a fly, and their fighting propensity, make them the most popular fly-rod salmon on the West Coast, and the one most similar in behavior to steelhead. And lucky me, I was going fishing for coho on the Lakelse River.

I drove down the highway along the blue Skeena, where I had a close view of the mountains known as the Seven Sisters. Then I found my way out to a lake and onto a logging road, and my tires began spitting gravel and mud. The river's name comes from the Indian *lax ghels*, "river of clams"—freshwater mussels, really. As I crossed a small bridge spanning the river, I saw fly anglers working in every one of the pools, and everyone seemed to be struggling with a fish on his or her line. This was simply incredible. Upon closer examination, I could see that the red-stained fish they were catching were not coho, but three- and four-pound pink salmon.

I drove a short way downriver and found a parking turnoff along the side of the road. A path through the woods took me down to a large gravel-and-sand bar where other anglers were fishing. Most of the men and one or two women I saw on the bank were heaving silver spoons on heavy spinning gear. The river was a bit murky, but I could see it was fly-fishable. A stocky fellow in a wide-brimmed hat with a huge feather in its band was reeling in a bright coho salmon.

"You're in luck," he told me as I approached. He had noticed my fly rod. "The river has just cleared up enough to fly-fish. It'll even be clearer by this afternoon. Me and my brother, we usually fly-fish here."

The aforementioned brother had a coho on his line, too. In fact the river was simply boiling with salmon. A fresh wave of coho had just taken up temporary residence in the pool. I felt as if I were in the middle of a wildlife documentary. Immediately above this deep pool, in a shallow gravel riffle, I could see scores of pink salmon paired side by side, holding their positions in the streaming water. I must have seen a hundred or more dark, wiggling shapes spread throughout the short riffle, their backs protruding out of what was only a few inches of water.

I stepped into the riffle, wanting to be as close as possible to these pinks; not so I could fish for them, but simply for the experience of walking among them. Salmon scattered at my feet as I crossed the shallow riffle. A few slapped against my legs as I waded through them. They moved off only a few yards, pairing off again immediately to resume their lovemaking. I don't think they would have stopped even for a hungry bear, so intent were they on the sexual act, blind to everything except the need to reproduce themselves. The males and females shuddered against one another like life loving itself.

The shallow riffle took me to the lip of the deep pool that was filled with coho. Unlike the badly discolored pinks, these coho were very bright, and I could see a great baitball of them milling about on the bottom. Occasionally, one would roll on the surface or leap into the air—a display of irritation or exuberance, I knew not which. For every one I saw rolling on top, or flipping into the air, I knew there were hundreds more salmon below them.

The coho shared the pool with dying pinks that had already spawned in the gravel above. In fact, there were so many spawned-out pinks in this pool that it was almost impossible for me to pass my fly through the water without snagging a dying fish. They drifted, only half-alive in the current, their life force ebbing away but their job done. Many carcasses littered the sandbar at the water's edge.

I chanced to look behind me on the bank and—oh, Jesus— here was this huge black bear heading our way. The bear wad- dled across the sandbar to this feast of dying salmon. He seemed as big as a small mountain. Every muscle under his black fir rippled as he moved toward us. It was the largest bear I had seen yet, much larger than the one I had encountered on the banks of the Morice River. The brothers had noticed the bear, too, and they began shouting at it, waving their arms. The bear stopped in his tracks to stare at us. One brother went for his bearstick, a bang stick that discharges loud claps to frighten away bruins. But the shouting and arm-waving sufficed. The bear turned and shambled off, disappearing into the under- brush. He would find a place to forage where there were per- haps fewer fishermen.

Salmon, bears, fishermen—what a scene. The salmon were pouring into the Lakelse as if delivering a message from the cosmos. The salmon had seen the world and now they were coming home. They were propelled upriver by a life force they had no capacity to reflect upon, let alone resist. Like the pinks, the coho would soon change color in response to their sexual urges. Having traveled the entire way, first down and then up the river of their births, these salmon could be said to embody the biological history of the Lakelse. Salmon spend most of their adult lives at sea, but the river is their cradle and grave. All Pacific salmon die after spawning, and this affects how we regard these creatures. The poet Ted Hughes spoke of a salmon "with the clock of love and death in his body."

No other fish has inspired such a deep and universal reflection as salmon. Salmon are mythopoeic. We offer salmon our prayers, songs, and poems. They in turn nourish our legends and our science. On the Pacific Coast of America, from northern California to Alaska, Indians have told tales about a great salmon spirit that dwells in the sea. Once a year this spirit puts on the mask of a salmon and returns to the land to sacrifice itself for the tribes. Most religions contain the theme of a tortured god: Christ dies for our sins; Prometheus is chained to the rock for stealing fire from heaven as a gift to mankind; Odin realizes that the greatest victim of sacrifice can only be himself. "There is a tortured god in every mythology," wrote the poet Robinson Jeffers, "and this seemed to me the fittest symbol to express something that is most beautiful and painful and true."

We share with the salmon a universe that is both divine and self-torturing. Salmon remind us that the world of living things is formed in pain and death. When we watch the spectacle of salmon returning from the sea, we are reminded again of the essentially tragic nature of life on earth. And we sense the world as being all the more beautiful for its dying.

I began catching pink salmon on every other cast. Most I foul-hooked. A few took the fly fairly, but there was little life left in those fish. How they managed to find the strength or interest to seize a passing lure baffled me.

I was using a 300-grain sinking line. The bottom of the pool was so sandy I wasn't hanging up. Coho salmon can be taken on floating lines, but only when they are very fresh out of the ocean. This far upriver, the coho probably wouldn't be inclined to take flies fished anywhere near the surface. I knew I'd get the best results by going deep. I stripped my line to speed up the retrieve, knowing that coho like a fly that is moved fairly briskly through the water.

In one pass through the pool, I felt a fish seize my fly and run away with it. Line peeled off my reel. I had on a very strong fish, that much was evident; I just assumed it was a coho. The salmon didn't leap, but made a very powerful downstream run. I really had to put on the brakes to check its flight. I'd reel in line and the salmon would retake it, making long runs that didn't seem to have any end to them. Finally I managed to steer this salmon over to the beach. One of the brothers, the guy in the feathered hat, ran thirty-odd yards below me to tail the fish.

"It's a big old dog salmon," he shouted, using the common term for a chum salmon. I saw that the dog salmon was in quite an advanced state of decay, with splotchy red-and-purple coloring all over its sides and back. If this was the kind of fight it put up in such a weakened condition, I wondered what a fresh chum would feel like.

"You foul-hooked it," the man in the feathered hat said by way of an explanation. A fish hooked in the tail can't be turned and is much harder to land. The brother slipped the hook and returned the dying salmon back to the river. "No wonder you had trouble beaching it," he said.

I felt another tug, and when I pulled up I had a small rainbow trout on the end of my line. There were resident rainbows in this river in addition to all the searun fish. I got another strike, and much to my delighted surprise, I reeled in a Dolly Varden, a red-spotted member of the char species which includes brook trout. These fish are now extinct in my home state of California. The next hookup brought me my first coho, a mere two-pounder, but as pretty as a freshwater pearl. Pinks, chums, Dolly Varden, rainbows, coho . . . this river had it all. I even had a chance of hooking up on a steelhead in this stream.

Coho salmon splashed and rolled around the top of the pool. As my fly passed along very near the bottom, I felt a few bumps, as if the coho were playing with the fly, perhaps teasing me. More likely the salmon were accidentally bumping it as they milled around on the bottom. I was fortunate I wasn't foul-hooking them. I continued to bring my fly back in short retrieves. I could see more salmon leaping at the far end of the pool below the sandbar. The salmon were all over the place now, and I suspected that new fish were coming into the pool, joining the salmon already there and forcing others to move upstream.

I felt a firm tug on the end of my line. A good-size salmon took off with my fly. There was no mistaking it—this time I had on a large coho. The fish didn't jump, but it ran upstream toward me. I reeled in frantically, only to have the salmon change direction and take the line back off my protesting reel. For one sickening moment I felt the salmon had come loose. But no, there it was, still on the line and securely hooked. I fought the coho two hundred feet to the sandbar and landed him. The salmon was still bright and very fresh, its skin opalescent. The cells underlying the skin that controlled pigmentation were only just beginning to trigger changes. Soon the silver haze on the coho would begin blending into a wash of pinks. I freed the hook and set the salmon loose to continue its journey upriver to spawn. That salmon had come a long way to get to this place.

The migration of salmon remains one of the planet's most sublime mysteries. Salmon arrive from oceanic journeys, navigating the Pacific by means of an internal compass within their brains, a kind of lodestone made up of millions of bits of iron magnetite woven into strands that apparently allow salmon to sense and follow the infinitely arcing grid of low-voltage current created by the earth's magnetic field. When salmon reach the continental shelf, their superior sense of smell allows them to distinguish their home stream from all the other freshwater rivers emptying into the Pacific. They have traveled thousands of ocean miles in search of a few square feet of river gravel. They seek the very pool that was their bassinet.

But no one really can explain fully how salmon form their extraordinary navigational sense. No one can say for sure how salmon, when the urge to mate suddenly comes upon them after years at sea, are able to call up a sense of their bearings relative to their home river. There are many theories, but no one has yet cracked the code. Both genetic and adaptive components seem to be at work. Salmon seem to be following instructions planted in their genes, but they are capable of adapting their behavior, too. Fry taken from British Columbia salmon stock and placed in a New Zealand river will return to the New Zealand river; not try to make their way back to British Columbia. This means that the migratory path itself isn't hardwired into the fish at birth, only the navigational system that gives them their spatial-temporal sense. Salmon aren't relying so much on an inherited sequence of directions as they are on an inherited capacity to "memorize" things. I am not speaking of memory in the cognitive sense—a salmon's brain isn't equipped to think. I'm speaking metaphorically. A salmon is able to "memorize" the particular mineral and chemical scent of its natal stream as it becomes imprinted on the salmon's odor receptors. This seems to occur when the salmon are very young and undergoing powerful hormonal surges affecting the thyroid gland.

Salmon swimming under the disturbance of the waves can hardly get a clear view of the sky and heavens. Yet there is some evidence that salmon can get a general sense of their bearings from the position of the sun and even the stars. Somehow salmon seem able to compare the rate of daylight change with latitude, although how this is done, no one can say for sure. It can't be a cognitive function, but rather something that gives the salmon an instinctive sense of its own position. The pineal gland in a salmon is covered by a thin area of bony skull that is so translucent it actually lets in light. This photosensitive organ, which has been called a "third eye," seems capable of taking in the angle of daylight and even moonlight. Think of a sailor taking a bearing at sea relative to the position of the sun and stars.

Somehow, as the earth's magnetic field shifts, salmon are able to adjust to changes in the angles of inclination and declination. The magnetic field not only moves with the seasons, it even changes slightly on a daily basis. Not only does the magnetic field shift, but the magnetic poles themselves wander. At the present time, the north magnetic pole isn't even found at true geographic north, but in Canada's Queen Elizabeth Islands. To complicate matters even more, the magnetic poles of the earth have actually reversed themselves eighty-two times over the past twenty million years. All modern salmon and steelhead descend from ancestors that somehow managed to find a way to adapt their migrations to these polar reversals.

When salmon leave their home rivers as youngsters and migrate out to their Pacific feeding grounds, they travel north along the continental shelf before turning westward into the Gulf of Alaska. But when the spawning urge comes upon them, and nature calls them back home after several years of feeding at sea, these salmon don't retrace their old routes back along the continental shelf. Rather they return by new, more direct sea routes. It is not known how they manage to call up a sense of their bearings.

Salmon, like many migratory animals, not only seem able

to navigate toward a goal by using an inborn sense of direction, they also seem to have an instinctive recognition of feeding grounds and resting places. No one knows exactly how these homing instincts work. But migratory animals seem able to recognize when they have arrived at an ancestral foraging or breeding ground. Monarch butterflies migrating two thousand miles south in the winter breed and die halfway through their migration, but their kin complete the migration. European cuckoos, whose eggs are deposited in the nests of other bird species, and who are raised by avian strangers, are capable of navigating back to ancestral feeding grounds in Africa without the aid of a parent or an adult bird to guide the way. And, of course, there are no salmon to guide the young back to their home streams, as all Pacific salmon die after spawning.

I don't know quite what to make of the migration and homing sense of salmon. There are forces out there that seem to govern behavior we don't fully understand. The more we observe, the more mysterious it all seems. Perhaps life is more mysterious than we give it credit for. Maybe the ultimate reality of life is unknowable from the standpoint of hard science. The fishes, the birds, and the animals all seem to be hearing notes in a music our human ears can no longer detect—if we ever heard that music at all.

In what is perhaps the finest poem in English since "Fern Hill," Ted Hughes described a decaying salmon resting like "a death-patched hero" in his birth river. "This is what the splendor of the sea has come down to," wrote Hughes in "October Salmon," an elegy about the loss of the earthly sublime. For

Hughes the river was a mirror reflecting the human condition. "So briefly he roamed the gallery of marvels!" Hughes said of that dying salmon, implying our journey as well. All about me were those death-patched heroes, horribly disfigured, sliding with the current, piling up in death at the river's edge. "So quickly it's over," wrote the poet. Regeneration lay upstream, in eggs buried under the gravel.

A SMALL MATTER OF ETHICS

THE NEXT MORNING I drove back to the Copper River, driving on past its junction with the Clore, and stopped to talk awhile with a trio of French fly-fishermen who were dredging the river with sunken lines. One of the things I had noticed about the visiting Europeans was that they all loved fishing with those heavy, sinking fly lines. Between my schoolboy French and their Clouseau-esque English, it was a wonder we were able to communicate at all. They told me they were staying at one of the German B&Bs in Terrace, and that each had caught a fish that morning.

I hiked downstream from the three dredgers. The river wound around a fairly lengthy spit of gravel, affording me a good stretch to wade and fish. No way would I use a sinking line on this river. That was too much like work. I tied on a big green-and-black streamer fly, and began my casting at the head of the pool. By the time I had progressed a third of the way down through the drift, I saw a sudden swirl just below the surface and felt a sharp tug on the end of my line. Physics teaches us that we are energy stored in the form of matter. I felt the energy of a steelhead run up the rod into my arm.

My rod dipped and recovered as the steelhead took the line in a burst of speed and jumped out of the water. The plunging and pulsing of a fly rod is one of the great tactile pleasures in fly-fishing. A fly rod in its tapered design is intended to be a particularly sensitive instrument. I think this feeling is what I like best about fly-fishing as a method. In addition to the grace of casting, there's that special *connection* to a fish through the limberness in the rod. A hookup is a kind of physical quickening.

The steelhead jumped in a shower of droplets. It shook itself on the surface, flipping and turning and twisting, and then it sounded. The steelhead began to saw back and forth below me in the pool. I lost and regained line in the back-and-forth contest. Ten minutes later I was pulling a seven-pound steelhead over to the beach for the release. It was a sleek and streamlined doe. I held the steelhead, marveling at the rose haze evaporating into the silver sheen. I slipped the hook out of the fish's jaw and held the steelhead in the current, allowing the oxygenated water to pass through the gills.

I rechecked the fly, making sure the barb on the hook was completely flattened. We use barbless hooks so we won't damage the mouth of a fish while releasing it. A fish with a torn mouth might not be able to survive. In fact, the faster a fish is released back into the water, the greater its chances of fully recovering from the exertion and the physical stress of the fight. Lactic acid builds up during these struggles and the result, if the fight goes on for too long, can be fatal. A barbless hook helps facilitate a quick release. I must stress that the purpose of the barbless hook isn't to minimize any pain a fish feels when hooked. We have little idea of what fish actually *feel* in the matter of pain, and we cannot presume to speak for them.

I wish that I could say here—much as in the disclaimer that appears in the closing credits of Robert Redford's film version of *A River Runs Through It*—that no animals were harmed in the writing of this book. But there's no getting around the cruelty in sport fishing. Any angler with half a conscience has to wonder what he does to a fish by hooking it. I've been fishing for the greater part of my adult life (the best part), and I confess to a certain degree of ambivalence when it comes to the infliction of pain on animals. And make no mistake about it—fishing is a blood sport, even when you practice catch-and-release. The cruelty isn't on the level of bear baiting or tormenting dumb farm animals in the bullring at Pamplona. But I have often wondered what kind of trauma a fish undergoes when it is hooked in the lip and "played" by a "sportsman."

Fish feel pain. All animals do, no matter how small they are. As Dr. Thomas Sholseth pointed out in an article published in *California Fly Fisher*, a magazine in which I sometimes publish fishing stories, even bacteria feel pain. Or at least they respond to it, and can be seen under the microscope trying to avoid irritants. But do bacteria suffer?

A trite question. But what about a fish? Fish have nervous systems, however primitive. As Sholseth explains it in his article, when a hook sinks into flesh, neurons at the hook site fire impulses into the spinal cord, and these discharge motor neurons that cause muscles to contract and pull away from the hook. Fibers in the spinal cord fire impulses up to the brain, causing the fish to flee, releasing hormones, and speeding up the fish's heartbeat.

But what does any of this mean to the fish? Perhaps not much of anything. After the hook is pulled out and the fish put back in the water, it seems to go back to its routine as if little had happened. That is if it doesn't die first from being mishandled.

When it comes to animals, we tend to anthropomorphize. We apply human characteristics and our own experience of the world to them. I know I do it all the time. But I'm a writer, and writers live and die by metaphor.

Scientists say that fish don't suffer—as we humans under-stand suffering, that is—because fish lack the necessary appa-ratus in their exquisitely small brains to process the elements and condition of suffering. In his article in *California Fly Fisher*, Dr. Sholseth pointed out that a fish's brain consists of nothing more than a simple brain stem. All the brain stem controls is eating and reproduction, and basic motor functions and reflex actions. Fish lack the cerebral cortex that is necessary for higher cognitive functions such as thought and emotion. Fish also lack an associative cortex, that portion of the brain that, as Dr. Shol-seth explained, translates raw sensations into feelings, reason-ing, and a full awareness of a given situation. A fish is equipped to avoid pain reflexively, but not to have thoughts about it, or to experience emotions or understand its condition.

In short, a fish lacks self-awareness. Suffering probably re-quires a sense of conscious awareness. Fish respond reflexively to pain but can't suffer because fish lack the necessary states of awareness for suffering to exist. In the long view, I suppose you could say that fish aren't even aware they exist at all. "I think therefore I am." Fishing makes us all Cartesian dualists.

Well, that explanation might make us feel a little better. But I'm not so sure I buy into it completely. Fish feel pain. I'm not so sure that fish don't suffer simply because they can't read *Ulysses*. (To be capable of that, they would know what true torture is.) None of us can be absolutely certain how another animal experiences reality. We can only view the world through the prism of human consciousness. The fact is we inflict some degree of physiological discomfort on these fish. Maybe more to the point, we are interfering with these animals as they are going about the business of being animals. We exhaust them through our sport, in a supposed contest between man and fish that really has only one outcome. Even the fish we release "unharmed" sometimes die from a buildup of lactic acid. I have done a lot of trout fishing in Yellowstone National Park, which functions as a virtual wildlife sanctuary, a place where animals are supposed to be protected from all forms of human interference. Yet we fishermen are allowed to yank trout out of the water in Yellowstone. This seems to me to be a contradiction (and one I intend to continue taking full advantage of with my fly rod).

Some animal welfare groups, such as Britain's Royal Society for the Prevention of Cruelty to Animals, and animal-liberation groups such as People for the Ethical Treatment of Animals (PETA), are actively involved in efforts to outlaw hunting and sport fishing. PETA, which espouses veganism, the most extreme form of vegetarianism, would also abolish commercial fishing on the grounds that humans don't need to eat animals of any kind, fish or mammals. PETA members have also discussed the feasibility of organizing acts of civil disobedience to disrupt anglers when they are on the water pursuing their sport, just as they have disrupted hunters in the field. Unlike most fishermen, I don't automatically dismiss these people as fanatics, although some of them may be. In fact I think the majority of them are highly principled people who raise legitimate philosophical questions about our treatment of animals. I also happen to think that they are well-intentioned but wrong.

I have read Peter Singer's *Animal Liberation*, the principal philosophical treatise for the animal-rights movement, and I kind of agree that sentient creatures are entitled to much the same ethical treatment as human beings. But my question is, what exactly is *"sentience,"* and when does an animal get it?

I have little problem with scientists using white rats in laboratory experiments. But I have a huge problem with them using chimpanzees and other higher primates. Gorillas, for example, have demonstrated that they might possess rudimentary language skills. Apes lack the vocal apparatus to speak, but through the use of pictures and objects, some primates seem capable of answering simple questions and communicating with us on a very rudimentary level. Their vocabulary comprehension might not be greater than that of a four-year-old human child—but we do not use small children as guinea pigs or as subjects for vivisection. Any primate that can use language to communicate has a cerebral cortex that allows it cognitive awareness of pain and suffering. I want to eliminate AIDS and other diseases as much as the next person, but I balk at torturing chimpanzees to find the cure. Likewise, I wouldn't use dogs for vivisection, because they seem to be able to interpret pain cognitively, fear it, and are capable of remaining traumatized long after the pain has been inflicted. Livestock seem to exhibit few if any of the symptoms of such trauma and fear as they are being led to slaughter, so I have no plans yet to become a vegetarian.

This doesn't mean that we can't improve the conditions of livestock in slaughterhouses and rearing pens or animals in research laboratories. I'm not so sure that animal liberationists didn't perform a public service when they broke into some of those research laboratories, videotaping evidence of terrible conditions and unnecessarily cruel treatment of the caged animals, conditions that frankly shocked the conscience.

But where I part with PETA is on their belief that all animals are sentient, and that all forms of animal life, or at least those animals that have nervous systems, are entitled to the same treatment as humans. I have said that we can never really know how another animal experiences reality and that science might not have the final word on everything. But science at least provides us with information that helps us to make certain informed deductions about life, certainly about the nature of animals and cognition. And it seems to me that if you accept the science behind the explication that a lower life form such as a fish can't really suffer because of the lack of a neocortex, then it seems to me that the arguments of the animal-liberationists fall short.

I have another problem with PETA, and not just with the tactics used by its members. I fully approve of nonviolent civil disobedience, and while acts of vandalism might be taking things too far, I remember that the Boston Tea Party was an act of vandalism, too. No, my objection to PETA is that, like the worst kind of church preaching, it is fundamentalist. Like fundamentalists everywhere—like anti-abortionists or Islamic revolutionaries—PETA members want to impose their moral vision of life on people who don't share that vision. It's one thing to advance your ideas and convert people to your cause through advocacy and public debate. It's another to impose your religion or moral philosophy on nonbelievers through the force of law—which is what PETA hopes to achieve by out-lawing hunting and fishing. From a public-relations standpoint, I suppose that disrupting hunters and fishermen in the field and on stream might be seen as a more acceptable form of protest than barging into luncheonettes and knocking corned-beef sandwiches out of people's hands—but remember that PETA's long-term goal is to get everyone to practice vegetarianism.

I suspect that somewhere in this anti-hunting and -fishing debate, a bit of class warfare goes on. Hunting is largely a rural pursuit. It's no coincidence that the organized movement against blood sports has made the most headway over in England, a country where there is very little left in the way of natural habitat, certainly nothing anyone would mistake for true wilderness. It's really town versus country in the U.K. The landed gentry traditionally has held shooting and fishing rights; the city classes, with good reason, resent this. In the United States, the PETA philosophy largely appeals to middle- and upper-class urbanites and suburbanites, and that new profes-sional class of Americans who, liberated by the computer modem and free to live anywhere they choose, are now moving into rural America in record numbers, bringing with them their cultural values and supposed greater sophistication. They enjoy living in the country, but not everything about country life appeals to their sensibilities. Certainly not the tradition the yokels have of shooting Bambi for dinner.

Another problem I have with the PETA philosophy is the idea that as humans we can somehow actually remove ourselves from the life-and-death struggle that makes up existence. We can't unlink ourselves from the chain of life; and all life is dependent upon death. In truth, we all have blood on our hands. Even vegans who wouldn't dream of so much as boiling an egg. If the whole world turned vegetarian overnight, we'd still have to kill a billion or so rats just to protect the granaries. Animal life perishes in agricultural production. When soil is tilled and fields are cleared or burned, small animals such as rodents die or are driven from their habitats. Countless numbers of insects perish, and we must count insects as members of the animal kingdom. (It has been estimated that each of us unknowingly consumes about a half-pound of insect matter annually, much of it, I suspect, in our salad.) Produce must be transported to market. This means petroleum exploration and oil production and motor vehicles, all of which kill wildlife, even those trucks transporting our vegetables to market. If you own a car, then you have done more to harm the environment than any duck-hunter ever has with his shotgun. Even the pets that we love and cherish force us to become killers. The innocent goldfish in his bowl lives on ground-up brine shrimp. It has been estimated that domestic cats kill at least a hundred thousand songbirds a day in the United States. This doesn't include the toll taken by feral cats, just our pets. This is infinitely more than the number of ducks and pheasants and other gamebirds shot legally by hunters in season. I suppose we could lock our cats in our apartments and never let them go outside (as some cat owners do, and as some bird watchers suggest), but then we would be denying cats the freedom to be cats. Every animal needs a chance to fulfill its animal nature. Maybe that's what humans can do for animals—allow them to be the animals that they are. Cattle and sheep don't live in the woods. Unless we're prepared to allow them to roam through suburbia grazing on our lawns, universal vegetarianism would condemn livestock species to extinction.

This isn't to say there aren't excellent reasons for becoming a vegetarian. It's a healthier option, and I fully plan to become one in the event that I survive my first myocardial infarction. Not only will I be healthier, but I'll be saving the Brazilian rain forest and slowing down global warming. But there just aren't any moral or ethical reasons for me to stop eating meat.

PETA has raised some important questions, however. And it's not my intention to make ad hominem attacks any more than it is to propound an apologia for fishing. I don't think there's anything I could say that would satisfactorily explain or justify my reasons for fishing to anyone from PETA. Certainly not that "*pain* versus *suffering*" argument. I fish because I like it—just as I'm sure many animal lovers are kind to animals because it makes us feel good. It might be as simple as that. I do what I love to do. And I have to take full responsibility for it. I sometimes ask myself what I would do if hard science proved conclusively that fish actually suffer. Would I quit, or keep on fishing? I suspect in my case, it would be the latter.

The oversimplifications of sport disguise a deep and unsettled ambivalence. I can accept the cruelty of killing only as long as I have a larger acceptance of the overall absurdity of life. Leo Tolstoy said the only thing we can know for an absolute certainty is that life is meaningless. Life is good, but death is certain. If you love the world, there are no happy endings.

I fish partly out of a sense of hedonism and pleasure. Food, drink, and sport are all part of what one might call the good life. But personal pleasure isn't a good enough reason to cause any animal pain. And so there has to be something more to it. In my case, fishing has given me the privilege of standing in some of the most beautiful places on earth. It has taken me from being a casual observer, to being a real participant. Fishing is my connection. For that reason, I'm unwilling to give up my sport. I don't want to lose all those things that go along with fishing, that special immersion into nature, that heightened avidity, that deeper way of seeing the world I live in. It never ceases to astonish me how one can experience a momentary transfiguration of spirit simply by standing in a few feet of water holding a fishing rod.

I drop the longest cast I can into the pool and feel the fly come around on the swing. There is a sudden tug on the line and I snap the rod upward. A solid weight comes to life and instantaneously the rod takes on the living energy of the steelhead. There it is again, that feeling of quickening, of liveliness, that comes with a hookup. I lose control of the line as the fish moves downstream at an alarming rate. This Copper River steelhead jumps once, twice, three times, and I think of how this fish is swimming out farther than any steelhead I have ever hooked. My rod takes a final, bucking plunge, and then springs back, inanimate. The feeling of liveliness has gone completely out of the rod.

There is something almost erotic in the act of hooking a fish. Now, I'm not saying it's as good as sex; I'm not that daft. But there is something deeply physical and enlivening at the moment of a hookup. I feel a curious mixture of physical gratification and moral ambiguity. There is even something writerly in the act, although I'm not quite sure what that is, or why it would be so. Much has been made of fishing as a contemplative person's recreation. For some reason, fly-fishing in particular is seen as something that comes dangerously close to being philosophical in nature. I've yet to mistake a trout stream for the School of Athens; and I know for a certainty that I've never had a profound idea while fishing. Yet somehow morality and art are all wrapped up in this pastime. For whatever reason, more has been written about fishing than on any other sport.

I checked my fly to see that it was still there, and then I resumed casting, directing my efforts straight across the water. There is something particularly pleasurable in fly casting. It makes you go all galactic. It's a form of emotional skywriting. You really lose yourself in the rhythms and enter into another state. Motions become particularly repetitive in steelhead fishing. Cast and step down. Cast and step down. The motion is repeated endlessly, until in time, several hundred yards of river somehow have disappeared, and you must walk back up the gravel bar to the head of the run and begin all over again.

I heard a *thock-thock* directly overhead and I looked up to see a helicopter flying low over the river. Possibly a heli-charter flying anglers up into the wilderness upstream. Or more likely the River Guardians on another aerial survey. I had met a few of the River Guardians the previous day, volunteers conducting an autumn angling survey on the Copper River. They were working for the Habitat Conservation Trust Fund, collecting data for B.C.'s Ministry of the Environment, Land and Parks. The purpose of the survey was to document the number of anglers who visited the Copper in the fall in order to get some idea of the steelhead catch rate and determine whether the fishing was improving or going to the dogs.

The extreme upper river had been designated Class One wilderness, and the only way to get there was to backpack or be dropped down by helicopter. I hadn't quite made up my mind about helicopters. They disturb the peace and tranquillity; yet they get you into places you'd never be able to fish otherwise. I decided that I approved of them. The helicopter disappeared, and once again I had the blue sky to myself. The River Guardians had asked me the other day how I rated my fishing experience on the Copper, and I told them it had surpassed my expectations. They asked me what I thought could be done to improve the fishing, and I said: "End the logging."

From where I stood on the gravel bar, I couldn't see the power lines that ran up into the hills, only the thick stands of spruce and fir. The logging road was hidden from view, too. I had the illusion that I was actually in the middle of a wilderness.

The American continent still feels new up here. In the United States most of us are rarely reminded anymore of just how fresh our continent actually is. You have to live in a place like Idaho or Montana to get an idea of that. I have sometimes wished, selfishly, that I had been among the first Europeans to lay eyes on it. But I've reconciled myself to the fact that I will probably never be the first to cast a line into any new and undiscovered place. The age of discovery is pretty much closed to us. At least geographically.

That night, driving back to Terrace on the highway along the Skeena River, tired but happy, fiddling with the car radio, I tuned in to a news program broadcast on CBC Radio. One of the great pleasures of driving in Canada is listening to the Canadian Broadcasting Corporation. CBC is the equivalent of our National Public Radio, but it is much more omnipresent and influential. You can drive across the entire length of Canada and listen to the commercial-free CBC broadcasts uninterrupted. As soon as the signal begins to fade, you can immediately pick it up on another broadcast band and never miss a beat. Out in the hinterlands, there is usually nothing else on. In some of the more remote areas, CBC is the only station you can tune in to.

That evening, the news was rather dismal. There had been a mass escape of penned Atlantic salmon on one of British Columbia's coastal estuaries. Escapements of farm-raised fish are not unusual, but this one was big enough to make the news.

Farm-raised salmon are big business. They are typically grown in net pens in saltwater estuaries. Hungry animals, like sea lions, try to get at the salmon, frequently ripping open the nets, and storms demolish them. Fish escape by the thousands.

These foreign farm fish become a threat to wild stocks. They mate in the same streams as the wild fish and compete with them for food. When genetically inferior farm fish mate with wild salmon, the result can be a biological disaster, as the wild genetic strain becomes diluted. Another problem is that Atlantic salmon, like the ones that had just made the spectacular break, are completely foreign to West Coast streams.

The year prior to my trip, a farm-raised Atlantic salmon rose to the fly of a fishing guide named Adam Tavender on the Dean River. The chaffed dorsal was unmistakable, clear evidence that the fish had escaped from an aquaculture pen and had somehow made its way up into one of the world's greatest trophy-steelhead rivers. Lesions on the fish made Tavender suspect disease or infection from parasites. Samples were sent for analysis to Canada's Department of Fisheries and Oceans. No one can say for certain what might happen to the Dean River's famous runs of steelhead if the searun rainbows suddenly have to begin competing with foreign escapees in their river. The fear is that the Dean's population of wild steelhead could be wiped out by a foreign intruder or by diseases associated with the penned fish, such as ulcerative dermal necrosis or infectious salmon anemia.

Because of the great concentrations of fish, food pellets, and fecal matter found in rearing pens, aquaculture has proven to be a great source of pollution. Pens that hold farmed fish become breeding grounds for massive infestations of sea lice. These tiny crustaceans are found in wild fish fresh from the ocean, but in very small numbers. But the pens concentrate the lice, allowing the infestation to grow to epic scale. Wild salmon and steelhead smolts heading out to sea and passing through the estuaries where the pens are kept can become as contaminated as the penned fish. The lice attack the gills and fins of the wild fish, and steelhead and salmon often find these parasites unbearable. Sometimes the sea lice kill the smolts. This kind of contamination can disrupt the migration cycle, as infected fish will turn around and seek relief back in fresh water, where the lice fall off, but where there is little food for the foraging migrants. Aqua farmers try to control the problem by treating penned salmon with chemical baths and food pellets containing lice medication. We, in turn, ingest the medicine and antibiotics when we dine on the fish.

Today more than half the salmon sold to consumers comes out of aqua farms rather than fishing nets. Ironically, the idea of aquaculture was sold to the public as a conservation measure by those who claimed that sea farming would relieve pressure on stocks of wild salmon that were being overfished. But today there is as much commercial fishing pressure on wild salmon as ever before. You don't grow farm salmon by watering them. It takes three pounds of ground fish meal to produce a pound of farm-raised salmon. The only thing that has changed is the increase in the worldwide consumption of salmon, once a luxury item. Aquaculture has made salmon more affordable to consumers.

As if the pollution weren't bad enough, scientists are now playing God and creating genetically engineered salmon. Biogeneticists in the Maritimes have bred a super salmon that grows twice as fast as normal salmon so it can be brought to market sooner. It's all part of the biogenetic gold rush taking place in laboratories and corporations worldwide, with little re-gard for the ethics involved. Humans have been practicing cross-pollination for centuries. But genetic engineering has made it possible for the first time in history for human beings to cross-breed different species, something that simply doesn't occur in nature.

Scientists have accomplished this rather dubious feat with Atlantic salmon. They have injected into farm-raised Atlantic salmon a gene from chinook salmon that produces growth hor-mone. Because normal salmon produce their growth hormone for only half the year, in warm-weather months, the scientists have injected a second gene taken from ocean pout that will keep the growth hormone kicking in all year. Now the salmon can grow to market size at twice the speed. If the biotech com-pany that owns the genetically modified salmon wins approval to sell its product, this super salmon could well become the first genetically modified animal to make its way onto our dinner table. (Genetically modified vegetables are already on our plates, although most of us don't know we're eating them.)

The great fear held by conservationists is that these geneti-cally engineered salmon will escape and breed with wild fish. This could wipe out wild stocks. Conservationists warn of something they call a Trojan Gene Effect. In some fish species, larger males tend to be more successful than smaller males in attracting females to breed with. With foreign DNA pumping growth hormone full-time, the genetically modified males could have an advantage over their wild salmon competitors. If the wild females preferred to mate with them, these pairings could produce offspring that are more susceptible to disease or have a harder time adapting to survival in the wild. Runs of wild fish could simply die out.

Scientists working for the company that wants to market this Frankensalmon are trying to allay fears of conservationists by promising to sterilize all salmon before they go into the net pens. As an added safeguard, all the salmon will be infertile females. This will eliminate any chance that a rogue male with a bullet in his gun might escape into the wild. These infertile domesticated salmon, the biotechnicians assure us, would have zero chance of breeding. Well, that's what aquaculturists said when sterilized grass carp were introduced into fish farms in Virginia. Now there are breeding populations of grass carp all over that state. The standard technique used in the sterilization process isn't foolproof, and has been known to leave some eggs fertile. Just remember what happened to those dinosaurs in *Jurassic Park*.

I'm not even sure I want to go fishing in the brave new world that is coming. Fishing allows us to connect momentarily with a creature from the wild and feel a spark of communicable energy. But in order to touch that animal we must also maintain a distance. There is an essential otherness, an apartness, in nature that we need to recognize and respect. But we seem to be approaching a time when we may never again be able to connect to a world that is truly wild. We are altering elemental processes of life on this planet, and it will be a sad thing indeed when we live in a world where there can be no escaping from ourselves. From biogenetic engineering, to global warming, to the ever-widening hole in the ozone layer, we are changing some of the most basic natural forces and balances around us.

It has been only a very short time since man began to change life on this planet with his Industrial Revolution. Once thought to be beyond our influence and control, nature instead has become subject to man's dominion.

Fish farms. Hatcheries. Smolts shipped downriver by barge to bypass dams. Genetically engineered salmon. Ours might be the last generation to know fishing in the wild, or a wild fish. A time may come when a child is born who might never know what a real fish feels like on the end of his line.

THE SHINING

WHEN I FIRST ARRIVED in B.C., Marilyn Quilley, who was doing a yeoman's job of trying to set me up with various lodge owners and outfitters, told me that the folks at Babine Steelhead Lodge were anxious to put me up at their place in the wilderness for a few days. Naturally I was delighted to hear that. Babine Steelhead Lodge had been a favorite of Joe Brooks and Dan Bailey. Brooks was the renowned fishing editor of *Outdoor Life*, and Dan Bailey operated a famous fly shop in Montana. Back in the 1950s, those two friends made annual trips to fish the Babine River. That was when British Columbia was still something of a frontier. The two men stayed in rustic cabins, one of only two lodges on the river back in those days. Tom Pero told me the pool fronting the cabins was one of the most beautiful on the river, and particularly suited to anyone who liked to fish with dry flies.

The only problem was that once Marilyn had secured that tentative invitation for me to come up there, she never heard from anyone at the lodge again. She was unable to get through to anyone by telephone. Apparently the lodge's only link to the outside world was by short-wave radio.

And so, not knowing what my itinerary would turn out to be, I decided to spend another day on the Copper River. John Fennelly had never fished the Copper, so I was one up on him there. He had also had miserable luck on his three Babine River trips, but that was only because he had gone too early in September, before the main runs of fish were in.

I drove up into the Copper River's canyon of pointed firs. The river appeared much cleaner than it had on the previous day. It washed over cobblestones and gravel beds, stealing cleanly through the deeper pools. The river broke down sky, forest, and mountains into myriad fragmentary images within the ripples. The valley was reflecting back in the distortions of light and shade on the stippled, flashing stream.

From time to time I would look up from my casting, my gaze traveling up the forested slopes and ridges, seeking the faraway mountain peaks. The steelhead heading upstream in search of their ancestral beds must have smelled those mountain peaks dissolved in the river.

After an hour or two of casting, a steelhead flashed with a half-roll on the surface and my line tightened. The steelhead felt heavy and strong, and when it jumped I saw a flash of silver that was as bright as the snowpeaks. The steelhead pulled line faster and faster. I raised the rod, and the steelhead changed direction, surfacing again, and then plowing several yards downstream into deeper water. I followed, hurrying along the cobble bar with my hands raised over my head, rod high, the reel protesting noisily. I could feel the weight of the steelhead all the way down into the rod grip. The reel spun; I reeled, trying hard to recover line. But the steelhead kept taking it out at an alarming rate.

The big fish exploded again, clearing the water and falling back on its side. It thrashed all about, wrenching and splashing. Fortunately there was no whitewater rapid downstream for it to escape into. I was pretty confident I would land this fish, if only I didn't screw up.

The steelhead changed direction and swam back upstream. I reeled line furiously to take up slack. And then the steelhead was pulling away from me again. It swam over sunlit cobblestones, boring into the green invisibility of deeper water.

We settled into a stubborn tug-of-war. The steelhead shook its head and flanks, twisted about underwater, and refused to submit. I was struggling with both the weight of the fish and the gravitational slide of the river. I didn't want the fly to pull out during the stalemate. That would be too heartbreaking.

Fifteen minutes later I was dragging twelve pounds of silver steelhead into the shallows. It was a wild and clean female, shining like a mirror. I held pure wiggling silver in my shaking hands, aware for the first time that I was breathing hard. The steelhead's colors were iridescent; rose and silver awash together. Dorsal and pectoral fins perfectly straight; this fish had never once brushed up against concrete. Here was a pristine fish, from a pure, unadulterated river race, a creature as clean and cold as the snowmelt water out of which it came. This was a steelhead as nature had intended.

The female had been on her way toward some life-giving tributary stream. Steelhead hold several months in the main river before swimming up narrow feeder creeks to spawn. They can spawn in amazingly shallow water, in creeks that are choked with brush and fallen logs. I was holding in my hands a miracle of perseverance. This steelhead had migrated from the deep ocean, wriggling over river rocks to create life. I looked up from the river to high, forested slopes beyond. And then I let the fish go, watching it shimmer off in the many sunlit refractions of the river, back on its way upstream, toiling toward the ragged mountains.

I drove farther upriver and found another good pool. The river swept around a wide bend in the gravel bar. I walked out to the head of the run, and discovered that the current was farther off from the bank than I thought. So I had to wade through a considerable amount of dead water in order to reach the current with long casts. I waded out as deeply as I dared and powered a cast in the direction of the fast-flowing water, my fly settling on the edge of the current. The fly moved only a few feet before a steelhead grabbed it without any visual warning whatsoever. The fish leapt once into the air and my rod dipped and jerked, pulsating with all the energy of the fish. And then the fly simply came free. Damn! That was over much too quickly. I don't mind losing a fish as long as I get a decent fight out of it. But that was over before it had even begun.

I waded a long way down the drift. The current came in closer to the bank and the casting became easier. When I saw a steelhead roll very near my fly, I almost lost my composure. I took a few unsteady steps backward over the cobblestones, nearly falling into the water, and cast to where I had seen the steelhead rise. Four or five casts more to the same spot, and I got another big swirl around my fly. I felt weight and tightened

MIST ON THE RIVER

up on the rod. The steelhead jackknifed out of the river and fell backward, sending up a heavy rain of spray. The racing fish nearly emptied the full line off my reel; the backing was beginning to show. I palmed the reel, slowing the steelhead's flight—but I couldn't turn the fish.

The steelhead circled stubbornly back and forth in a bull-dogging fight. It slapped the water with its shovel tail, sending up more spray. It thrashed and tore around as my rod quivered and danced. I tried to put a short rein on the fish, but the steelhead was still too green to be brought to shore. My rod dipped dangerously, and I put on even more pressure. The steelhead shook its head and spat out the fly. Where once there had been a thrashing steelhead, there was now only flowing water.

I sat down on a rock to eat a sandwich. Another angler was walking across the wide gravel bar directly toward me. He had two fly rods; one in his hand, and the other stuffed down the back of his parka. The rod tip at his back stuck out like an antenna. This guy was loaded for bear. He walked straight over to me. So far, I'd been the only fisherman working this drift. If this had been California, there would be a mob on this gravel bar, all fighting for position, never budging from their chosen spot in the river.

"Do you mind if I fish here?" the man asked.

There must have been three hundred yards of gravel bar and empty river. And yet, God bless him, he was afraid he might disturb my fishing. He wanted to know if I would mind if we shared the immensity of this pool. I couldn't get over how polite people were up here. This fishermen was like most Canadians

I had encountered on my trip. If I had to choose a single word to describe the people who lived north of the forty-ninth Parallel, that word would be *nice*. Everyone was kind and amiable and considerate to the point of self-parody. I don't think I heard a single car horn blown in anger the entire time I was in B.C.

"Please, wade in anywhere you like," I told him.

"How have you been doing?" The man with two fly rods seemed genuinely interested in what my answer might be. One rod was lined with a floater, the other a sinker. He wouldn't have to take time away from his fishing to switch over.

"I've had a pretty good day so far," I told him. "I hooked three and landed one. How have you been doing?"

"I landed two fish." The man told me he was from Prince George and he made it a point to visit the Copper River every autumn. He was even thinking of moving to Terrace after he retired.

The fellow waded in upstream, leaving me the virgin water below. We fished for an hour, and nothing happened. And then my neighbor was suddenly into a fish. His steelhead began jumping crazily, somersaulting into the air, and the fellow's fly rod began to dance up and down with manic energy. The steelhead twisted and turned before making a burning run downstream. The man followed with his jerking fly rod.

Finally the angler appeared to wear down the fish. He led it over to the cobble bar to tail it. But when the steelhead saw the angler, it panicked and simply went crazy. For a minute I thought he was going to lose his fish. It thrashed, lunged, and flipped all around, splashing the angler several times. Finally the fisherman managed to bring his catch over to the bank, where he could tail it. He struggled to hold the fish still, to keep it from banging itself to death on the rocks.

"Nice fish," I called over. Surprisingly, it wasn't that large. Maybe six pounds. But it had put up a terrific scrap.

I resumed casting. Steelhead never come easily. But when they do get in a mood to take, they can be very democratic about it. A steelhead is just as likely to inhale a poorly-cast fly as one presented with a lifetime of skill and experience behind it. I know that isn't fair, but life isn't fair, either. I depend on that unfairness.

A long time went by while I waited for the hard jolt of a steelhead. And just when I thought that it might never happen again, a broad head rose out of the river and engulfed my fly. I restrained an impulse to tighten up too quickly, dropping the short loop of excess line that was in my hand. That line disappeared up through the rod guides, and I felt a self-tightening weight.

I raised my rod smartly. The steelhead jumped and ran down and across the river, my fly line slicing behind it. The steelhead made another picture-perfect leap, and then sounded. I tried to hold him, fighting against the power of the fish as well as the weight of the flowing river. Line began coming off my reel again, and the steelhead made a third jump, splashing and flinging spray. The steelhead took a few more yards off my line, but I managed to turn and hold him. The steelhead tugged and pulled with mighty shakes of its head and body. It flipped and twisted all around. But I held fast.

The steelhead now settled into the current, refusing to

budge. For a time it remained immobile, too heavy for me to horse in. But then its strength began to fail. Rod high, I waded downstream, taking in line. I held the rod even higher to keep the fish's head out of the water, and led him toward the shore. It was at this moment that the hook pulled free and the fish came loose. My battle cry—*"Shit!"*—caused the other angler to look up from his fishing. We both laughed.

I checked my fly to make sure that the hook hadn't pulled straight—it was okay—and then I resumed casting. Each cast was one more chance to hook up to a steelhead, and another chance to appreciate the splendor of the Copper River sliding over river stones. A light breeze loaded the canyon with the sharp fragrance of Sitka spruce. It was easy to empty my mind into this river. When you are fishing you are no longer merely an observer. You are actually doing something that feels vital. This kind of action has a way of absorbing you into the picture.

I changed flies, cast, and mended. I could see the sunken fly moving above the cobbled bottom. And then I lost sight of it. As the line was swinging around nicely, it came suddenly tight, and I pulled up on another steelhead. I could feel the throb of the fish a split second before it exploded out of the water.

The steelhead twisted in midair and crashed back into the river. It jumped again, getting some nice hang time at the top of its arc. It fell back, rose a third time, and skipped away downstream. At first there was no stopping this fish. I listened to the line coming off my reel.

I put on the pressure and managed to check the run. The steelhead came to the surface, and the water around it boiled. I pulled as hard as I dared, and the steelhead gave way a little.

We went back and forth, the steelhead and I. I started to work it over toward the bank—only to have it suddenly race downstream, taking off more line and scaring the wits out of me.

They say that you remember trout mostly in the numbers you catch, but that you remember every single salmon or steelhead you have ever hooked. This was certainly true in my case; but perhaps only because I had caught so few of them. Check back with me in about twenty more years. But for every steelhead I managed to hook, each seemed to have its own personality and its own unique way of fighting. Just look at the way that six-pound fish pulled that other angler all over the river. No two steelhead I ever caught acted quite the same.

The steelhead made another boiling rise to the surface. This steelhead would be fighting on to the bitter end. Just as I managed to bring the shining chrome steelhead over to the bank, it panicked, flinging spray at me. The steelhead raced off, drawing yards of line as it ran. But it was in a weakened condition now, and the fish no longer had the steam for a really long run. I had little difficulty checking the steelhead's escape. With the rod straining between us, I brought the fish over to the beach, threw down my rod, and grabbed hold of the fish with both hands.

I held a henfish of about ten pounds, a silver beauty touched by a rainbow haze. I removed the hook and let the sleek steelhead slip back into the river. She disappeared into her crystal element. Where she was bound, I knew not. What she was experiencing in the cold splendor of her river, I couldn't say. They do not know love, and if they did, we would not be worthy to receive theirs. The sight of that sunlit fish disappearing into the Copper River is still with me.

When I got back to the Cedars Motel that evening, I turned on the Weather Channel to check out the long-range forecast. A low-pressure-system cold front was heading into northern British Columbia. It looked as if it was going to bring plenty of rain and maybe even some snow. That was something I didn't care to hear. So far I had lucked out on the weather. But things were changing fast.

I was still waiting for some word from Babine Steelhead Lodge. Each day that passed made the prospect of getting a cabin on the Babine appear less likely. I really wanted a taste of that wilderness river. The Babine was a tough river to get to, tough to navigate, tough to wade. But it was a river known for truly awesome steelhead, some of the largest in British Columbia. Babine steelhead are not ordinary steelhead by any means. Steelhead that swim that far into the interior of British Columbia grow slowly and mature late. Because of their long residency in both fresh and salt water, many of those fish would be making their first spawning run at the age of seven years. For some reason, when Babine fry are transplanted into other rivers, they only grow to ordinary size. But an unusual number of bucks in the Babine exceed twenty and even thirty pounds.

I knew that the really good fishing on the Babine would begin around the middle of October, which was two weeks away. Truly hard-core Babine steelheaders stay through November, which is really like winter this far north. It would be interesting to see the river in that bleak season of hoarfrost and bare cottonwoods, with a pale sun tracking low on the horizon, just over the mountains. The evergreen forest would be a snowy dream world then. It really would be lovely to experience the Babine in such a bitter season.

There were no paved roads along the Babine. The river ran through trackless forests of evergreen. The Babine was official wilderness. Provincial regulations forbade logging anywhere within three kilometers on either side of the river. The Babine's whitewater rapids could be treacherous, and the river is always a challenge to boat. In places, the Babine is simply unnavigable, and boaters have to get out and portage.

I studied a Forest Service map of the river. The map showed a dirt logging road that would take me into the upper Babine. It would be a long, bone-jarring drive. Maybe take half the day to get there. But from the logging road, I'd be able to fish a mile or so of the Babine where it flows out of Babine-Nilkitkwa Lake. Babine Lake is the largest natural body of fresh water in British Columbia, and because the river is lake-fed, the Babine runs clean most of the time, although it can be affected by glacial runoff from the Nilkitkwa River.

The only problem was that foot access to the Babine was limited to about a mile of river. And, strictly speaking, that part of the river really couldn't be considered a true wilderness experience. There was the real possibility that a lot of anglers who had driven up there would be jockeying around for room on a limited number of pools. Such fishing might be unpleasant and disappointing. I wasn't so sure I wanted to experience the Babine River under those conditions, at least not on my first trip.

In any event, the weather forecast didn't sound promising. And I had to get back home to San Francisco, where I had commitments. Perhaps it would be better to wait and see the Babine another time. Maybe the first sign that one is maturing as an angler is that you know when to stop, even when you're having the best fishing of your life.

EPILOGUE

As I write this, rain is falling hard on San Francisco. It is winter, and the steelhead rivers are rained out. I am sitting at a desk stacked with piles of reports bearing such titles as *Steelhead Restoration and Management Plan for California, International Symposium on Steelhead Trout Management,* and *Summary of the Third Pacific Coast Steelhead Management Meeting.* And the fourth, the fifth, and the sixth such management meetings. California Trout, an environmental organization dedicated to the protection of trout and steelhead rivers, has provided me with such brochures as *Summer Steelhead,* which deals with the Middle Fork of the Eel River, and *The Model Steelhead Stream Restoration Project,* for the South Fork of the Trinity River. And I confess that I don't quite know what any of this adds up to.

Sport fishermen, lodge owners, guides, and fisheries biologists—everyone I spoke with—seemed to think that the Skeena steelhead fishery was on the upswing. After all, unprecedented numbers of steelhead came back into the Skeena in 1998, almost seventy thousand fish, the highest "escapement" in the forty-five years since people began keeping records. The following year, the year of my trip, somewhat fewer steelhead returned, a little under forty thousand fish, but still the fifth-highest return on record. I heard a rumor that a fly-fisherman on the Sustut River caught and released a thirty-four-pound steelhead, which would have beat Karl Mausser's record. Those fabulous returns of steelhead were mostly attributed to restrictions on commercial fishing, such as the removal of the nylon salmon nets at the mouth of the Skeena River. Natural cycles were at work, too: climatic and oceanographic factors, such as warming and cooling sea currents and shifting ocean temperatures, which affected survival rates at sea. Core samples taken off the floor of Alaskan tidal estuaries have shown us the larger picture. In *Passage to Juneau*, the author Jonathan Raban met quite by chance with marine biologists who were tracking salmon migrations in the Inside Passage. By sinking tubes into the soft inlet bottoms and searching the contents for scales, bones, phosphorous, nitrogen, and other trace elements that dead salmon leave behind and which had washed out from the rivers, the marine biologists were able to determine that the yearly fluctuations in the size of the runs were of little significance compared to variations that occurred in between decades over several centuries. By examining core deposits dating back all the way to the European Middle Ages, the scientists told Raban that Alaskan salmon populations have regularly waxed and waned over time. The salmon population might crest for a decade, at most, only to plunge downward again. Those shifting patterns seemed somehow to be linked to fluctuations in warm and cold ocean currents. By plotting a graph, one could see the natural fluctuations in the salmon population seemed little affected even by the steady downward decline that began with the onset of commercial fishing off the Alaskan coast in the mid–nineteenth century. It was entirely possible that salmon and steelhead populations in British Columbia were merely cresting again as part of a natural cycle.

I don't want to dismiss or minimize the environmental dangers posed by overfishing. After all, the cod fishery off the Grand Banks of Canada, once the world's richest fishery, collapsed completely because of overfishing, annihilating not only the cod but wiping out the historical fishing culture of the Maritimes. Unfortunately, our technology now enables us to fish faster than fish can reproduce. There's always the danger that something very much like the collapse of the fishery on the Grand Banks could happen in the Pacific Northwest. But I think it is more likely that if salmon and steelhead depart from British Columbia, it will be on the backs of lumber trucks.

Meanwhile, most everyone connected to the sport fishery in the Skeena region seems to think that conditions are improving overall. The fishing guides and lodge owners all told me this, citing effective conservation measures, restrictions on commercial netting, and overall improvements in the sport fishery as proof that things are getting better. And they probably are. The improved runs of salmon and steelhead in the Skeena give us every reason to be optimistic.

But I'm not an optimist. I take a much longer and more tragic view of history and life. I'm not going to go into detail about all the dangers steelhead face in the modern age. That would require another kind of book from the one I have written. Suffice it to say that in the fullness of time, the steelhead will lose. Wilderness will shrink. The land will be tamed. That's the direction history takes us in. I think it's highly doubtful that humans and steelhead can continue to live together in the future. One of us will have to go, and we know who that will be.

A tragedy of the human race is that we sometimes forget that we are animals. We are only a part of a larger animal kingdom. All the other animals are waiting for us, waiting to see if we are going to destroy their world while we are hungrily consuming our own. The steelhead are waiting on our every move.

Steelhead connect us to a more primal and, in some ways, more authentic world. I only wish more people understood this and felt this. But there aren't enough people out there willing to think of salmon and steelhead in the same way they might regard condors or snow leopards. In the minds of most people, fish lack the necessary charisma and glamour. The American bald eagle was brought back from the edge of extinction because it stood for something, because it was regarded as something unique to the American experience. In the Pacific Northwest, the steelhead stands for something unique, too. It is a kind of synecdoche, a small part of an experience that stands for the whole. Salmon and steelhead are to the Pacific Northwest what lions are to the Serengeti.

John Fennelly was a bit of a pessimist, too. In *Steelhead Paradise*, he lamented the fact that British Columbia was going to change. He wrote: "Within another decade or two, most of its primeval charm is certain to disappear." Still, I think he would have enjoyed seeing his rivers as I saw them. I know I did. There's still a lot of primeval wilderness worth fighting over, worth protecting, worth saving.

I find it enormously gratifying to know that the final interview ever published with Ted Hughes, Britain's poet laureate, and perhaps the greatest English-language poet of our time, appeared not in a newspaper or a literary journal, but in a fishing magazine. After the suicide of his wife, the American poet Sylvia Plath, and the ensuing scandal and recriminations, Hughes made a habit out of avoiding the press. But in an act I thought particularly fitting for a poet who had written a volume of verse called *River*, Ted Hughes consented to be interviewed by Tom Pero for *Wild Steelhead & Salmon*. Pero met Hughes through his gregarious correspondent, Ehor Boyanowsky, the professor of criminal psychology, whose fly-fishing article had so outraged Maxine Douglas. Boyanowsky had met Hughes at a poetry reading in Vancouver, and the two became fast friends. It was Boyanowsky who hosted the poet laureate on his first-ever steelhead fishing trip, to the Dean River. Hughes wrote his famous poem "The Bear" while sitting on the banks of the Dean. In the poem, Hughes described how the river, temporarily in flood, carried off a cache of wine from the camp, and swept the corpse of a grizzly bear downriver.

The interview that Hughes granted to Pero was published in the winter of 1999, not long after the poet's death from cancer. In his lengthy conversation with Pero, Hughes spoke with great feeling about what salmon and steelhead fishing had meant to him as an artist. Hughes adored Atlantic salmon fishing, and financial and literary success gave the Yorkshireman of once-modest means the opportunity to fish salmon rivers in his native England, and in Scotland, Ireland, and Iceland, as well. He had gone to Alaska to fish for king salmon, and in more recent years Hughes had gone on trips to fish for steelhead in the Dean

River. In that final interview, Hughes referred to the steelhead as "a more intense form of salmon." Hughes described to Pero how fishing had informed his art and contributed to an inner life of the imagination. His fishing experiences, he said, drew him ever more deeper into the world. When speaking about salmon, Hughes referred to something he described as "this huge appeal of the hidden watches." And he spoke of "the fascination with flowing water and living things coming out of it—to grab at you and be grabbed." Yes, I thought, as I read that remark, that about sums it up perfectly. Fishing is a fascination with moving water and the life that leaps out to seize and be seized.

Hughes also said that he didn't think salmon and steelhead could survive our times. They were too valuable to be allowed to live, he said. "We're cashing in the whole globe, aren't we?" Hughes said. "How can wild salmon escape?"

By traveling to British Columbia, to the northernmost range of the steelhead, I had found a fisherman's paradise—but one that has been threatened by the fatal pressures of our times. I don't know how long British Columbia will be there for us to experience. That is, the British Columbia that I saw, and which John Fennelly wrote about. With any luck, it will remain pristine and wild for some time yet. With luck, I hope to make many more trips to British Columbia. And I hope to go to Alaska, too, and even Kamchatka, where I might find the last truly unspoiled steelhead wilderness on earth. My great hope is that I get to see this vanishing world before it is gone.

At the conclusion of *Steelhead Paradise*, John Fennelly wrote: "While there are still large areas in the Skeena Valley virtually untouched by the hand of man, it has seemed worthwhile to put down on paper some account of the beauty of the country, and the pleasures it holds for a fisherman." I have felt the same way.

I am not a polemicist. I have no illusions about reversing the course life takes us on this planet. I'm not writing about steelhead in order to save them; I know my book will change nothing. I write only to be a witness to what is here and what is changing. Ours might be the last generation to know wild, unspoiled fishing. The loss is not to us who have fished, and who can always return to our rivers, if only in our memories. The real loss is to those unborn who will never know what we have known.